*The*
*SELF-*
*COACHED*
*RUNNER II*

The

SELF-

COACHED

# RUNNER II

*Cross-Country and the
Shorter Distances*

By Allan Lawrence
and Mark Scheid

*With a Foreword by Fred Wilt,
Purdue University Women's Coach,
Cross-Country and Track and Field,
and an Afterword by Tom Tellez,
1984 U.S. Olympic Sprint Coach*

LITTLE, BROWN AND COMPANY • BOSTON • TORONTO

FIRST EDITION

Before embarking on any strenuous exercise program, including the training described in this book, everyone, particularly those with known heart or blood-pressure
problems, should seek medical clearance from a physician,
preferably one with sports medicine experience.

*Library of Congress Cataloging-in-Publication Data*
Lawrence, Allan.
   The self-coached runner II.
   Includes index.
   1. Running—Training.   2. Running races.   I. Title.
GV1061.5.L38   1986        796.4′26        86-15357
ISBN 0-316-51674-0
ISBN 0-316-77302-6 (pbk.)

RRD VA

*Published simultaneously in Canada*
*by Little, Brown & Company (Canada) Limited*

PRINTED IN THE UNITED STATES OF AMERICA

*For Mary, Troy, and Claire.*

M.S.

*For Mary G. and Roy H. Cullen, whose love and support of running are exceeded only by their commitment to the improvement of the physical well-being of all individuals.*

A.L.

# CONTENTS

# FOREWORD

VERY FEW OF US RUN far or fast for the simple joy of physical movement. Many run reasonable distances at comfortable speeds for reasons of recreation and health. It requires minimal knowledge of training to accomplish the health and recreational aspects of running. But for those who desire to race fast over specific distances, much more knowledge and effort are needed.

In all probability, human physiology and body structure have not changed for millions of years. But knowledge of human physiology and scientific justification for training routines as they are known today have increased to a nearly incalculable degree, especially during the current century.

Eminently qualified and experienced authors Allan Lawrence and Mark Scheid have combined their clear understanding of physiological training principles in a logical, commonsense, straightforward blueprint that leads the self-coached runner in a step-by-step progression to his or her specific, measurable racing objective.

I genuinely regret that I did not have the benefit and direction of training knowledge available in this book during my own competitive days as a self-coached runner.

Fred Wilt
Purdue University Women's Coach,
Cross-Country and Track and Field

# ACKNOWLEDGMENTS

A NUMBER OF PEOPLE HAVE contributed to the growth of *The Self-Coached Runner II*. Among those we would like to single out are Bert Nelson and Jon Hendershott of *Track and Field News*. A variety of expert technical advice and comment came from Boots Garland, Ray Stanfield, Steve Straub, Victor Lopez, Kirk Baptiste, Carl Lewis, Bill Collins, J. Fred Duckett, and especially Tom Tellez and Fred Wilt. James McLatchie coaches a number of the athletes whose achievements are recorded here, and we would like to thank his runners and all those whose pictures appear in these pages. Contributing photography was provided by Robert S. Cozens, Conrad J. McCarthy, and Bruce Glikin.

The weight-training program on pages 21 and 22 is a compilation of several prepared for university-level athletes by strength specialists Keith Irwin and Jeff Madden. Our thanks are due to Glenn Ballard, Headmaster, Kinkaid School, for the use of the school's track facilities. The staff of Little, Brown did its usual fine job of preventing us from splitting infinitives as often as we split lap times.

To Dr. Herbert L. Fred — runner, writer, and friend — we owe a debt that goes back for years and transcends even the worlds of running and writing. Thanks, Herb, for everything.

A.L. and M.S.
Houston, Texas

# INTRODUCTION

THIS BOOK IS WRITTEN FOR the thousands of runners across America who are interested in learning to run in track, cross-country, or short road-race competition. Among you are veterans of dozens of longer road races who want to explore new facets of speed and endurance competition, high school and junior high athletes just getting started in competitive running, and professionals in corporations large and small who have responded to the challenge of Corporate Cup competition at the local, regional, and national levels.

Our goal in this book is to provide runners who have these new interests with the information they need. Our first book, *The Self-Coached Runner*, tells a road runner what he needs to know to train and race well at distances of 10 kilometers and beyond. Much of the information in that book would have been provided by a first-class professional coach — if the runner had access to one, as most do not. Additionally, we hoped that, by providing the runner with the *reasons* he should do a given workout, as well as with the workout itself, he would eventually learn to coach himself much more competently than he could before.

This book is a sequel of sorts to *The Self-Coached Runner*, applying similar principles designed for the growing number of runners who want to diversify their running experiences and explore areas such as track racing and cross-country competition — events that can seem very much like road racing but that often turn out to have major differences to the runner new to them.

Many professionals in the field reported our philosophy and practical advice in *The Self-Coached Runner* to be a valuable guide. We hope that cross-country and short-distance coaches — beginning and experienced — will find this book equally valuable in assisting them to design, test, and support their own ideas and coaching theories.

The first chapter of this book explores the ways you can find out what your "best distance" is — the distance you are physiologically best suited to run, the distance at which your training will pay the greatest dividends. As we* make clear there, the odds are about two to one that *your* best races will *not* be the longer ones. Instead, using your own racing experience, computer tables, common sense, muscle biopsy, or the simple table we provide, you can determine whether you need to change your racing habits and consider an event that better fits your physiology.

The second chapter discusses the philosophy and practice of track training: how it differs from road racing in its demands on your body, what abilities you need to develop, and how to find your best track event. The succeeding chapters deal with the specific training necessary for maximum performance at the various track and short road distances. Chapter 3 discusses the sprints: 100 meters, 200 meters, and the 400-meter run (once considered a middle-distance event but now the longest of the sprints). Chapter 4 focuses on the 800-meter/half-mile distance. Chapter 5 discusses what many consider the queen of individual track events, the 1,500-meter/1-mile run. Chapters 6 and 7 provide information and schedules that allow the runner to train for competition at the long track (or short road) distances: 3,000 meters, 2 miles, 3 miles, 5,000 meters, and 5 miles (8,000 meters).

Chapter 8 introduces you to the special world of indoor track — what aspects of your outdoor training will carry over, and what modifications you need to make. In Chapter 9 we examine cross-country, a sport that has roots in both track and road racing. The similarity to road racing is obvious; cross-country events tend to be the same length as the shorter road races, rarely farther than 10K. Road-race training will not let you run your best races on cross-country courses, however, because cross-country can be as much a *power* event as an endurance event, and so the techniques and power

* Throughout the book, "we" and "our" refer to both authors, "I" and "my" to Allan Lawrence.

training that carry over from the track pay real and important dividends.

The Glossary contains information you need when you're making the transition to track and / or cross-country racing. Some is basic — what high school track runners might learn during their first season. But if you haven't had that first season, whatever your age, and don't have teammates around to fill you in, this section will. Other information given here is the type that often no one seems to know in detail; everyone knows, for example, that you should race in the inside lane; you have to run farther if you run one lane wider. How much farther? (8 meters on a standard outdoor track.) Is it ever smart to give up that yardage? (Sometimes.)

Like its predecessor, this book is designed to act as your coach and to train you to coach yourself. We hope that it opens a new world of running for you to experience and enjoy — the world of cross-country and the shorter distances.

*The*
*SELF-*
*COACHED*
*RUNNER II*

*Power running: the lead pack in the 1986 World Cross-Country Trials. (Photograph by Conrad J. McCarthy)*

# ONE

# Finding Your Distance

WHAT'S YOUR BEST DISTANCE?

That's a very common question among runners, but the truth is that most of America's thirty-five million competitive runners don't really know. They run on the roads because that's where most of the races are. They run 5Ks and 10Ks and occasional marathons because those are the races that are available to them, the races "everybody" runs.

But a little elementary logic shows that many road racers enter the wrong events: 99 percent of the road races in this country are longer than 3 miles. Studies by physiologists show that races at these longer distances are run most efficiently by athletes with more than 60 to 70 percent slow-twitch (ST) muscle fibers. Similar studies have also determined that the ratios of fast-twitch (FT) to slow-twitch fibers are distributed in a bell curve across society; that is, only 20 to 30 percent of all runners have the right ratios to run their best races at 3-plus miles. And because your fast twitch / slow twitch ratio is genetically determined and fixed at birth, training doesn't modify it.

The conclusion seems inescapable: As many as twenty-five million of America's road racers may be running the wrong event. They simply have the physiological tools to run better in shorter races — distances usually run on the track.

In a sense, the evidence was always there to see. If the FT/ST ratio is distributed in a bell curve across society, and if training can't modify it, it would be logical to expect that the same percentages would hold true for elite athletes — in other words, only about 30 percent would run their best race at over 3 miles. The other 70 percent, physiology predicts, would find their best events among the shorter distances — and they do: In the Olympic Games, of all the running events, nineteen (79 percent) are less than a mile in length; only the marathons, the men's 5,000- and 10,000-meter runs, and the women's 3,000 are longer.

## What Are ST Fibers and Why Are They Doing These Terrible Things to Me?

Physiological studies divide muscle fibers into two groups. The slow-twitch fibers, as their name implies, contract more slowly (less than half as fast, in fact) than the fast-twitch fibers. And they do not contract as strongly. They make up for this by being well supplied with capillaries and by having a high oxidation potential, so they can maintain efficiency in contraction over a long period of time and can be used continuously with less fatigue.

Fast-twitch fibers contract quickly and strongly but are relatively low in oxygen supply, so they fatigue more easily. Physiologists further break fast-twitch fibers down into two different types: $FT_a$ and $FT_b$. The difference between the two may not be of much importance to runners, except that $FT_b$ fibers seem to have even more FT characteristics than $FT_a$ fibers, being more dependent upon glycogen and less upon oxygen; they are also smaller than $FT_a$ fibers.

If you are among those twenty-five million road runners with less than 70 percent ST fibers, you may have your greatest potential as a cross-country or track runner. The history of the sport is full of stories of runners who moved from mediocrity at one distance — or even at another sport — to greatness at the right distance.

Ruth Wysocki, who showed early promise in the half-mile and mile races, after several disappointments took to the roads, where she found herself highly competitive. Returning to the track in time for the 1984 U.S. Olympic Trials, she combined her half-mile speed with her newly developed road-racing strength and upset Mary Decker in the finals of the 1,500 meters.

Kirk Baptiste furnishes another example. When he came to work

*Joan Egan ran several disappointing marathons before taking four national medals in her first track competition. (Photograph by Bruce Glikin)*

under Coach Tom Tellez at the University of Houston, he was one of the top high school quarter-milers in the nation, and everyone expected him to continue to race at that distance. Why argue with success? But to Tellez, who has one of the world's best eyes for technique, Baptiste's natural distance appeared to be at the shorter sprints. After a year of training in sprint technique, Baptiste had gone from a pretty good college quarter-miler to a silver medalist at 200 meters in the 1984 Los Angeles Olympics.

As we can see from this last example, the best advice a runner can have at choosing his or her distance could come from a knowledgeable coach.

But as we discussed in our last book, most of America's competitive runners don't have a coach. How do you determine what your best distance is?

*MUSCLE BIOPSY*

Traditionally, the most accurate method of determining fast twitch/slow twitch ratio is through muscle biopsy. Under local anaesthetic, a small incision is made through the skin, a hollow needle is inserted, and a section of muscle is removed. This muscle core can be analyzed and a fairly accurate ratio of fast-twitch fibers to slow-twitch fibers can be determined.

In athletes, it is customary to do the biopsy on a muscle that is not ordinarily used in their sport. Biopsies of runners are often done on upper arm muscles. The fast twitch/slow twitch ratio can vary a bit from muscle to muscle — those muscles used in endurance work, like the soleus of the lower calf, have a higher percentage of slow-twitch fibers; muscles used in power running, like the quadriceps (along the front of the thigh), have a lower percentage. Because of this variation, it is important that the muscle chosen for biopsy accurately reflect the athlete's overall musculature.

Muscle biopsy does not sound like a very pleasant procedure, and runners report that (contrary to what they had been told) it hurts, too. Nevertheless, it is the most accurate way to discover FT/ST ratios, and it is a standard part of the testing procedures of highly structured national track programs, such as those of East Germany and the Soviet Union.

## FINDING OUT BY EXPERIENCE

Muscle biopsy is a fairly recent development in the world of running, and so you might suspect that there must have been other, earlier methods used to find an athlete's best distance.

In fact, muscle biopsy initially served only to confirm empirical evidence of a runner's choice of distance. The runners of the past learned their distances "the hard way": by training for and racing all of them as they proceeded through their athletic development in junior high and high school. Carl Lewis, for example, didn't know that he was going to be a world-class sprinter when he joined his first track team. He ran everything up to the mile (without significant success in any event) until well along in high school — several years after he first started racing — when he settled on the 100 and the long jump; experience at a number of distances had shown him that his greatest potential lay there. For Bill Rodgers, it was mediocrity at a number of track distances that led him to move onto the roads, where he found greatness.

Most of today's millions of "average" road runners, of course, never had this early exposure to short distances. They race on the roads like everybody else; their contact with the track is limited to a track workout once or twice a week; or they may do no track work at all.

## COMPUTER TABLES

Even for this generation of road runners, there are ways to discover your best distance without the pain of muscle biopsy or the emotional trauma of re-experiencing high school. One of these is through the use of computerized evaluations of your best times at various distances.

These "computer tables" are extrapolations of the scoring tables used in calculating the relative merit of the various events in the men's decathlon and the women's heptathlon. Because it is difficult to know from mere observation whether a vault of 14 feet is "better" or "worse" than a shot put of 46 feet, the multi-event tables were designed to give a point value to the entire range of possible jumps, throws, and runs in the decathlon and heptathlon. Thus, judges of the multi-events can find that a 14-foot vault is worth X points and a shot put of 46 feet is worth Y points. The tables reveal not only which is better (or higher-scoring) but also how much better it is.

When applied to the various distances at which races are run, both on the track and on the roads, this principle makes it possible to compare your best 10K time, for instance, with your best marathon time and determine which was the better race — the one that scores more points on the computer tables.

If you are an experienced road racer, you will have a number of races to look up. You may also want to consider the range of times you have run at a given distance, from fastest to slowest (after throwing out the catastrophes like the times you walked in — or were carried).

As you are doing this, a pattern should begin to emerge. Does your "typical" marathon time get a higher score than your usual time in the 20K or half-marathon? Does your half-marathon usually beat your 10K? If so, it's a good indication that you are physiologically better suited for the longer distances; that is, you have a relatively high percentage of slow-twitch muscle fiber. You might want to consider training for the ultra-distances like 50K and 50 miles to achieve your full potential.

On the other hand, if the reverse pattern becomes obvious — if your short-distance times consistently score higher than your long-distance times — you are probably not as well suited physiologically for the longer runs as you are for the short ones. If your 10K is better than anything else, you will want to try racing at shorter distances.

One important note: If your chart peaks at 10K and drops off in both directions, that may not necessarily mean that 10K is your best distance. Consider what type of training you've been doing. If you're doing road-race training, that training is going to help prepare you for distance running, no matter what your FT/ST ratio is. Races shorter than 5 miles, especially races of 5K and less, require specific training for you to reach your potential in them.

*Shorthand formula.* To give you a shorthand method of making comparisons of your best times at various distances, we have included a brief table that will let you get an idea of your best distances. When using it, please remember that it is designed to serve only as an approximation to guide you in your race selection, not as a real scoring table. Additionally, races at different distances are affected differently by weather: Sprinters run better in warm weather, but runners at distances over a mile are slower in the heat. Wind slows all runners, unless they are running with it.

To use the table, put an X on your best time for each event (if your time falls between two times on the table, mark between them). Connect the X's so that your times make a line across the table.

Then, since all the race times in a horizontal line are roughly equal in quality, the top of your line marks your best effort, and the events around that peak may be your best distances.

For example, if you've run 17:19 for 5K, 36:50 for 10K, and 5:01 for a mile, you will want to experiment with training and racing distances from 2 to 5 miles. *Don't* think that because a 17:19 5K is equal on the table to a 12.0 100 meters and a 1:16 20K, you should be able to run those times too. If you can, you haven't reached your potential at any distance yet, and you'll need to train and race more before your best distance begins to emerge.

## ON RACE AND RACES

In the United States, a remnant of racism affects track events. Put simply, it is this: If you're white, you must be a distance runner; if you're black, you're a born sprinter. Often there is pseudophysiological mumbo jumbo offered to "back up" this assertion — blacks are "more muscular" and have "longer thigh bones"; whites have more "discipline." It boils down to "blacks are more physical, whites are more mental," the old canard that leads to black wide receivers and white quarterbacks in football.

This racism is not just antiblack, of course; it may make mediocre quarter-milers out of potential great black distance men, but it also produces mediocre white milers who ought to be running 200s. We are conditioned to believe that the Black = Sprinter/White = Distance Runner dichotomy is true because that's all that we see . . . in America. But a look at the rest of the world will show us that it's just not true.

White sprinters have dominated the Olympics and world records for the last twenty years. Russian great Valery Borzov won two golds in the 1972 Games in Munich (100, 200), while Alberto Juantorena took the 400 and 800 at Montreal in 1976, setting a mark in the for-

TABLE TO DETERMINE "BEST DISTANCE"

| 100m<br>100y | 200m<br>220y | 400m<br>440y | 800m<br>880y | 1,500m<br>1 mile | 3,000m<br>2 miles | 5K<br>3 miles | 8K<br>5 miles | 10K<br>6 miles | 20K<br>10 miles |
|---|---|---|---|---|---|---|---|---|---|
| 10.0<br>9.25 | 20.4<br>20.5 | 45.5<br>45.9 | 1:44.9<br>1:45.6 | 3:36.9<br>3:55.1 | 7:49.6<br>8:27.0 | 13:33.8<br>13:04.0 | 22:22.9<br>22:31.3 | 28:24.2<br>27:21.8 | 59:30<br>47:13 |
| 10.2<br>9.39 | 20.7<br>20.8 | 46.2<br>46.6 | 1:46.6<br>1:47.3 | 3:40.5<br>3:59.0 | 7:57.7<br>8:35.7 | 13:48.0<br>13:17.7 | 22:46.5<br>22:55.1 | 28:54.3<br>27:50.8 | 1:00:34<br>48:04 |
| 10.4<br>9.59 | 21.2<br>21.3 | 47.4<br>47.7 | 1:49.5<br>1:50.3 | 3:48.2<br>4:05.9 | 8:11.8<br>8:51.0 | 14:12.8<br>13:41.5 | 23:27.8<br>23:36.6 | 29:47.0<br>28:41.5 | 1:02:26<br>49:32 |
| 10.6<br>9.77 | 21.6<br>21.7 | 48.4<br>48.8 | 1:52.0<br>1:52.7 | 3:52.2<br>4:11.7 | 8:23.7<br>9:03.9 | 14:33.7<br>14:01.7 | 24:02.7<br>24:11.7 | 30:31.4<br>29:24.3 | 1:04:01<br>50:47 |
| 10.8<br>9.95 | 22.0<br>22.1 | 49.4<br>49.8 | 1:54.5<br>1:55.3 | 3:57.8<br>4:17.8 | 8:36.2<br>9:17.4 | 14:55.6<br>14:22.8 | 24:39.3<br>24:48.6 | 31:18.2<br>30:09.3 | 1:05:40<br>52:06 |
| 11.0<br>10.13 | 22.4<br>22.5 | 50.5<br>50.9 | 1:57.2<br>1:58.0 | 4:03.6<br>4:24.1 | 8:49.3<br>9:31.6 | 15:18.8<br>14:45.0 | 25:17.9<br>25:27.4 | 32:07.4<br>30:56.7 | 1:07:25<br>53:28 |
| 11.2<br>10.33 | 22.9<br>23.0 | 51.6<br>52.0 | 2:00.1<br>2:00.9 | 4:09.8<br>4:30.8 | 9:03.1<br>9:46.9 | 15:43.1<br>15:08.5 | 25:58.5<br>26:08.3 | 32:59.3<br>31:46.6 | 1:09:15<br>54:55 |
| 11.4<br>10.50 | 23.3<br>23.4 | 52.6<br>53.0 | 2:02.6<br>2:03.4 | 4:15.2<br>4:36.7 | 9:15.4<br>9:59.9 | 16:04.8<br>15:29.1 | 26:34.9<br>26:44.9 | 33:48.7<br>32:33.8 | 1:10:54<br>56:14 |
| 11.6<br>10.68 | 23.7<br>23.8 | 53.7<br>54.1 | 2:05.4<br>2:06.3 | 4:21.4<br>4:43.4 | 9:29.1<br>10:14.7 | 16:28.9<br>15:52.6 | 27:15.1<br>27:25.4 | 34:37.1<br>33:20.7 | 1:12:44<br>57:40 |
| 11.8<br>10.87 | 24.1<br>24.2 | 54.8<br>55.2 | 2:08.0<br>2:08.9 | 4:27.3<br>4:49.8 | 9:42.4<br>10:29.0 | 16:52.3<br>16:15.0 | 27:58.3<br>28:08.9 | 35:27.2<br>34:09.2 | 1:14:31<br>59:04 |
| 12.0<br>11.07 | 24.6<br>24.7 | 56.0<br>56.4 | 2:11.2<br>2:12.1 | 4:34.0<br>4:57.2 | 9:57.7<br>10:45.7 | 17:19.4<br>16:41.2 | 28:39.6<br>28:50.5 | 36:25.0<br>35:04.6 | 1:16:35<br>1:00:42 |
| 12.2<br>11.24 | 25.0<br>25.2 | 57.0<br>57.4 | 2:13.8<br>2:14.8 | 4:39.9<br>5:03.6 | 10:10.9<br>10:59.9 | 17:42.7<br>17:03.6 | 29:18.6<br>29:29.7 | 37:14.8<br>35:52.5 | 1:18:21<br>1:02:06 |
| 12.4<br>11.42 | 25.4<br>25.6 | 58.1<br>58.5 | 2:16.6<br>2:17.5 | 4:46.0<br>5:10.2 | 10:24.7<br>11:14.8 | 18:07.0<br>17:27.0 | 29:59.3<br>30:10.7 | 38:06.9<br>36:42.7 | 1:20:13<br>1:03:34 |

| | | | | | | | | | |
|---|---|---|---|---|---|---|---|---|---|
| 12.6 | 25.9 | 59.2 | 2:19.4 | 4:52.3 | 10:39.0 | 18:32.5 | 30:42.0 | 39:01.5 | 1:22:10 |
| 11.60 | 26.1 | 59.6 | 2:20.4 | 5:17.1 | 11:30.4 | 17:51.5 | 30:53.7 | 37:35.2 | 1:05:06 |
| 12.8 | 26.3 | 1:00.3 | 2:22.4 | 4:58.9 | 10:54.1 | 18:59.2 | 31:26.8 | 39:58.7 | 1:24:12 |
| 11.79 | 26.5 | 1:00.8 | 2:23.5 | 5:24.3 | 11:46.8 | 18:17.1 | 31:38.7 | 38:30.3 | 1:06:43 |
| 13.0 | 26.7 | 1:01.4 | 2:24.2 | 5:05.0 | 11:07.9 | 19:23.6 | 32:07.8 | 40:51.4 | 1:26:05 |
| 11.96 | 26.9 | 1:01.9 | 2:25.3 | 5:30.9 | 12:00.8 | 18:40.6 | 32:20.0 | 39:20.7 | 1:08:21 |
| 13.2 | 27.1 | 1:02.5 | 2:28.1 | 5:11.0 | 11:23.0 | 19:49.9 | 32:55.2 | 41:48.2 | 1:28:09 |
| 12.15 | 27.3 | 1:03.0 | 2:29.2 | 5:38.1 | 12:17.8 | 19:06.4 | 33:07.7 | 40:15.8 | 1:09:45 |
| 13.4 | 27.5 | 1:03.6 | 2:31.1 | 5:18.2 | 11:38.0 | 20:17.0 | 33:37.6 | 42:46.1 | 1:30:12 |
| 12.33 | 27.7 | 1:04.1 | 2:32.2 | 5:45.3 | 12:34.3 | 19:32.0 | 33:50.3 | 41:11.3 | 1:11:26 |
| 13.6 | 28.0 | 1:04.8 | 2:34.0 | 5:24.7 | 11:52.4 | 20:43.6 | 34:22.0 | 43:44.0 | 1:32:15 |
| 12.51 | 28.2 | 1:05.2 | 2:35.1 | 5:52.4 | 12:50.5 | 19:57.6 | 34:35.3 | 42:06.3 | 1:13:02 |
| 13.8 | 28.4 | 1:05.9 | 2:37.1 | 5:31.5 | 12:08.6 | 21:11.3 | 35:08.9 | 44:43.0 | 1:34:24 |
| 12.70 | 28.6 | 1:06.4 | 2:38.2 | 5:59.9 | 13:07.4 | 20:24.3 | 35:22.2 | 43:03.8 | 1:14:44 |
| 14.0 | 28.9 | 1:07.1 | 2:40.2 | 5:38.7 | 12:24.8 | 21:40.4 | 35:57.8 | 45:45.6 | 1:36:39 |
| 12.89 | 29.1 | 1:07.6 | 2:41.4 | 6:07.6 | 13:24.1 | 20:52.2 | 36:11.5 | 44:04.0 | 1:16:31 |
| 14.2 | 29.3 | 1:08.3 | 2:43.5 | 5:46.1 | 12:41.9 | 22:10.7 | 36:48.9 | 46:51.2 | 1:39:00 |
| 13.08 | 29.5 | 1:08.8 | 2:44.7 | 6:15.7 | 13:43.6 | 21:21.4 | 37:02.9 | 45:07.1 | 1:18:21 |
| 14.4 | 29.7 | 1:09.3 | 2:46.3 | 5:52.2 | 12:56.1 | 22:36.0 | 37:31.6 | 47:46.0 | 1:40:58 |
| 13.24 | 29.9 | 1:09.9 | 2:47.5 | 6:22.4 | 13:59.0 | 21:45.8 | 37:45.9 | 45:59.7 | 1:19:54 |
| 14.6 | 30.1 | 1:10.4 | 2:49.1 | 5:58.6 | 13:10.9 | 23:02.4 | 38:16.0 | 48:42.9 | 1:43:01 |
| 13.41 | 30.3 | 1:10.9 | 2:50.3 | 6:29.4 | 14:15.0 | 22:11.1 | 38:30.6 | 46:54.5 | 1:21:31 |
| 14.8 | 30.6 | 1:11.8 | 2:52.8 | 6:07.0 | 13:30.2 | 23:36.8 | 39:14.1 | 49:57.5 | 1:45:42 |
| 13.62 | 30.8 | 1:12.3 | 2:54.1 | 6:38.5 | 14:35.8 | 22:44.1 | 39:29.0 | 48:06.1 | 1:23:38 |
| 15.0 | 31.2 | 1:13.2 | 2:56.6 | 6:15.7 | 13:50.3 | 24:12.8 | 40:15.1 | 51:15.6 | 1:48:32 |
| 13.84 | 31.4 | 1:13.7 | 2:57.9 | 6:48.0 | 14:57.8 | 23:18.8 | 40:30.4 | 49:21.4 | 1:25:51 |

(This table is prepared from times given in *Computerized Running Training Programs*, by James B. Gardner and J. Gerry Purdy, published by Track and Field News, Inc., Los Altos, California.)

*Pietro Mennea running his world-record 19.72 seconds for 200 meters. (Photograph by Joe Arrazola, courtesy* Track and Field News)

mer of 44.26, the fastest time ever at sea level. Even with the modern dominance of the sprints by black American greats like Carl Lewis, Kirk Baptiste, and Calvin Smith, the world 200-meter record (19.72 seconds) is still held by Pietro Mennea, an Italian.

Similarly, no one can doubt the ability to excel at the distances demonstrated by dozens of great African runners, beginning with Abebe Bikila's marathon gold medal in Rome in 1960. Since then the Kenyans, led by Henry Rono, and the Ethiopians, of whom Miruts Yifter may have been the best, have set a number of records and won world cross-country crowns. Currently the nation that holds the world marathon championship is Djibouti, a tiny African nation (with a population of 360,000) that boasts three marathoners with times under 2:11.

In summary, great sprinters are great because they have the ability and do the work, and the same is true of great distance runners, although the work is different. It's not the color of your skin, or any physiological quirk related to race, that determines whether you're a sprinter or a distance runner.

## GETTING STARTED

Whether you use muscle biopsy or computer tables or any rule of thumb, if you find that you seem to have race potential at the shorter distances, you will certainly want to explore a variety of shorter-distance events. Even without discovering your best distance, you may want to compete at short races anyway, because you're in high school or you're involved in Corporate Cup events. Finally, you may simply want to explore the world of track racing for the best reasons of all: Track training and racing will teach you something about running and about yourself — and it's fun.

# TWO

# The Philosophy and Practice of Track Training and Racing

INCREASINGLY, RUNNERS WHO "grew up on the roads" during the running boom of the seventies are moving toward the track as a race venue. Some may have decided from experience — or been told — that their talents lie in the short distances; others may have made that determination by a more scientific analysis through muscle biopsy, or by using the computer tables we discussed in the last chapter or the formulas given there. Still others may have merely been touched by the age-old curiosity, "Just how fast *can* I go?"

When you decide to become a track man, or at least to explore a running world that has challenges and rewards as rich and varied as those of the road-running world, there are two points you need to keep in mind.

*Mileage.* If you are a longtime road racer, you probably have a well-established sense of how many miles a week you *should* run, and if your weekly mileage drops below that, you feel that your training is falling off. But when you convert to track training, your mileage is almost certainly going to drop (although the intensity of the workouts will increase). If you attempt to stretch your mileage up toward your old road-running level while maintaining the intensity of your track work, you will burn yourself out.

*Fatigue.* You are also going to be tired in a different way. As a road runner, you are used to a small amount of residual fatigue, which may make you feel a bit heavy-legged or, in more advanced cases in marathon training, may make you think there's a small piano on your shoulders. Doing track training, you usually won't *feel* tired. You'll know you're overtrained perhaps only when you try to run a quarter in 72 seconds and can barely squeeze out a 78. In short, you can't go by the feel for training you developed in road running; you have to develop a new feel for the track.

## Weight Training

There is little doubt among top coaches that sprinters need good upper-body strength to sprint effectively. They give various reasons for this: (1) Sprinting is a power event; therefore the runner benefits from more power. (2) It's not the power so much as it is being strong enough to maintain form at the end of a hard sprint; weaker runners get tired, their form falls off, and they slow down. (3) Sprinting, like all running, has a substantial psychological component; the main effect of weight work is that the runner *feels* stronger, so he runs stronger — the sprints are short enough so that he won't pay for his stupid, aggressive, macho actions as he would in a marathon.

Whatever the reasons — probably a combination of these — it is no accident that Carl Lewis gained fifteen pounds during the year he went from being one of the best sprinters in the country to being the best in the world. Or that Jarmila Kratochvilova, the former world-record holder in the women's 400 meters, has obviously benefited greatly from improved muscular strength.

There are a variety of types of weight training available to the aspiring runner. Each has its virtues and its limitations.

*Free weights* is the term usually applied to any variation on bar-bell/dumbbell equipment, in essence a pipe with a circular weight at either end, even when plastic-, chrome-, or gold-plated. To some extent free weights fell into disuse when more sophisticated (and less dangerous) equipment became available and was purchased by

Short-distance runners often augment their power and increase their speed through weight training. (Photograph by Conrad J. McCarthy)

gyms, athletic departments, and professional teams, but free weights have a number of advantages.

First, they are relatively inexpensive. A beginning set (around 110 pounds) costs less than fifty dollars. Used sets are even cheaper and are widely available in garage sales as New Year's resolutions wane. So, as a beginning sprinter, you can get a start on your upper-body development — as the ads say — in the privacy and comfort of your own home.

Second, free weights work muscle groups in conjunction with each other, instead of isolating a single group in each exercise. While isolation has its advantages, training groups together has benefits, too, especially since in sprinting your whole body will be working toward the same goal.

However, there are also drawbacks to using free weights. The first comes because they are free. Since the only thing controlling them is you, and since a weight workout is designed to fatigue the muscles, there may come a time when you have less control over them than you should. Then you can get hurt: a muscle strain, a sprain, even a broken foot if you drop them.

Also, the apparent simplicity of free weights is sometimes deceiving, for to be used correctly and safely, free weights often need more equipment than you have available. It may be tempting to use a coffee table for bench presses (lying on your back on the table and pushing the weights straight up from your chest), but coffee tables may collapse from the extra weight and leave you flat on your back, trying to catch a hundred pounds of iron. Even if the table takes the extra strain, consider that you may be too tired to lift the weights the last time and get out from under them. If you're going to do bench presses, use a weight bench.

In addition, to be used correctly, free weights require good technique. If you don't know how to bend your knees and get your hips low to pick up a barbell, for example, you could injure your back. So heavy free weights are best used only by people who know what they're doing or by people being watched by a good weight coach.

Unless you fall into one of these categories, you should keep your free weights relatively light, under 50 pounds or less if you're small or weak. You can get an excellent workout with free weights of this size; the plus is that high repetitions with less weight produce extra strength with less added muscle bulk and weight — a case of getting stronger while staying light.

*Universal* systems are characterized by a series of pulleys lifting a stack of weights, which slide up and down in an enclosed frame. Instead of adding disks onto the bar, you control the amount of weight by inserting a metal pin at the desired point in the stack. The availability of several different stations around the machine, and several different sets of pulleys, makes it possible for you to exercise a wide variety of muscle groups. The major advantage of this method is that the weights are not free, and even a dropped bar will cause no more than a loud noise (and perhaps a cracked weight). The stations provide some degree of muscle isolation and make it less likely that you will do an exercise "wrong." Universal systems are costly enough that the best models are found in gyms and health clubs. (Some smaller home models have appeared recently; if you want the advantages of this type of training at home, be sure to check these for sturdiness and number of stations provided.) The primary drawbacks to Universal training are the cost and the lack of adjustability in some systems, which can limit the effectiveness of your training.

*The Nautilus type of equipment* combines the pulley system with a series of cams that vary the resistance of the weights in the stack according to the relative strength of the muscle at a given point in its contraction. This, in theory, increases the amount of improvement you can expect from a given workout. Additionally, these machines usually allow for a range of adjustment in seat and bench placement so you can work your muscles through a full range of contraction. The main limitation is that each machine is usually designed for only one exercise, so a full set becomes expensive and takes up a lot of space.

*Which type of equipment should you use?* Use what is available. We runners tend to be an introspective, reflective lot. We can spend hours and days debating the relative merits of two different running shoes, two different vitamin supplements, two different training schedules. In spite of the fact that running is a very low-tech sport, we are always hoping for a high-tech solution, alert to the most recent innovations, looking perhaps for the magic key which will let us run that 5 percent faster we feel is *there,* if we could only get to it.

We sometimes forget that we are more likely to gain that 5 percent if we buy one pair of shoes *or* the other, put them on, and run. The same is true of weights and most other equipment. A week of workouts lifting a portable typewriter in a case will do more for your running than a week of waiting for your new equipment to be delivered. As a practical matter, too, you have easier access to one type of weight training or the other. Finally, *how* you use the weights is more important than whether you have machines or barbells.

*Weight-lifting technique* can be summarized in a few common-sense rules that will work for you no matter what your ability or strength:

- Warm up and warm down. Work up a light sweat with mild exercise — calisthenics or stationary bicycle and stretching — before lifting; warm down by stretching.
- Don't pile on too many weights. You should be able to do between 8 and 12 repetitions in any exercise, having to work a little on the last 2.
- Don't lift too often. Total workout time should be about 30 to 45 minutes no more than three times a week. Allow at least 24 hours between workouts.
- Don't overspecialize. Do an exercise for each of the major muscle groups: lower back/buttocks, legs, torso, arms, abdominals.
- Don't go too fast. During each repetition, count *two* while lifting the weight, count *four* while letting it go back. Exhale throughout, then inhale moderately before the next repetition.

The last rule is probably the one most often broken. Too many runners take the term pumping iron literally and pump away, no doubt feeling that they're doing more good for themselves by moving the weights quickly — after all, *running fast* is better training than running slowly, so the same must be true for weights. Besides, it looks a lot more impressive to toss all that mass around.

A little reflection may help convince you that it doesn't work that

way in weight training. Quick acceleration of the weights uses the
$FT_b$ muscle fibers, the same ones that give you explosive speed.
"Great," you may reply, "I need all the explosive speed I can get."
The problem is that the fast-twitch fibers aren't very trainable, and
that means you can pump iron quickly for a year and not be much
better off at the end of that time.

Even worse, once you've accelerated the weights quickly, they
tend to complete the exercise on momentum. That means that your
slow-twitch muscle fibers — the ones that *are* trainable — get an
easy ride. So they don't get the full benefit of the workout either.

It's easy to tell that it is harder to lift and return weights slowly
than to pop them up and down. Additionally, the fibers that are now
getting the work are the ones that can benefit most from your lifting.
So if you spend the time with weights to help your running, slow
down and let them work.

## A WEIGHT-LIFTING PROGRAM

Once again, there are a variety of programs available. Most of the
good ones use the basic principles outlined above. If you don't have
one you like or don't have one at all, here's one that works:

### WEIGHT-TRAINING WORKOUTS

| | Sprinters (up to 400 meters) | Middle-Distance (800 meters– 1 mile) | Distance (2 miles and up) |
|---|---|---|---|
| WARM UP and STRETCH: | 10 minutes | 10 minutes | 10 minutes |
| 1. Bench Press | 3 sets of 10 | 2 sets of 10 | 2 sets of 10 |
| 2. Parallel Squat | 3 sets of 10 | 3 sets of 10 | ——— |
| 3. Power clean | 3 sets of 8 | 3 sets of 8 | ——— |
| 4. Pullover | ——— | (optional) | 1–2 sets of 10 |
| 5. Leg Curl | 3 sets of 10 | 3 sets of 10 | ——— |
| 6. Lateral Pull-down | (optional) | (optional) | 2 sets of 10 |
| 7. Hammer Curl | 3 sets of 8 | 3 sets of 8 | ——— |
| 8. Preacher Curl | ——— | ——— | 2 sets of 10 |
| 9. Lateral Raise | ——— | ——— | 1 set of 10 |
| 10. Vertical Hip Lift | 2 sets of 15 | 2 sets of 15 | 2 sets of 20 |
| 11. Bench Sit-ups | 2 sets of 20 | 2 sets of 20 | 2 sets of 20 |
| 12. Back Extensions | ——— | ——— | 1 set of 15 |
| STRETCH: | 5 minutes | 5 minutes | 5 minutes |

To perform a bench press: Lying on your back on a weight bench, push weights straight up to full arm extension. Return.

Parallel squat: Feet should be shoulder-width, weights on shoulders. With head up and eyes straight ahead, bend knees and squat until your thighs are parallel with the floor. Return.

Power clean: Feet and hands should be shoulder-width. Squat and lift weights, bringing them up smoothly in front of your body to shoulder height, raising up on your toes as they pass your chest. At top of exercise, rotate elbows under weight bar so that you are ready to push weights up over your head. Instead, lower them smoothly to the ground, reversing the procedure.

Pullover: Lying on your back on the floor with weights at arm's length behind your head, bring weights over your head and finish by your sides; keep arms straight.

Leg curl: Usually done on a machine. Legs are moved from straight position to almost completely bent with heels close to buttocks.

Lateral pull-down: Usually done on a machine. Reach up and grab bar over head, pull straight down to chest level.

Hammer curl: A curl done with dumbbells held like a hammer; your thumbs should be up.

Preacher curl: A curl done at a bench that allows you to rest your upper arms on a padded support and move only your lower arms.

Lateral raise: Raise dumbbells from your sides up to shoulder height; keep wrists and elbows slightly bent.

Vertical hip lift: While holding yourself off the ground with straight arms, either from parallel bars or a hip lift chair, raise straight legs to horizontal level.

Bench sit-ups: Sit-ups done on an inclined bench; keep knees bent.

Back extensions: Lying face down with legs secure and hips slightly elevated, move upper torso up from floor and return.

---

This program is designed to be used during the noncompetitive season, when you are building strength. Once competition starts, it is a good idea to modify and in some cases eliminate the weight program, in the same way that you will change your track training as you near the date of your main season.

## What Do You Do When You Reach Your Time Goal?

A major problem for competitive runners is holding their edge after reaching or surpassing a time goal they have set for themselves.

There is no hard and fast rule, unfortunately, for how long you can maintain this edge; your age, your experience, your commitment, and your psychological approach to competition determine how many weeks in a row you can race successfully.

The self-coached runner who focuses on a particular time goal and regards this as the pinnacle of her season may find herself psychologically flat after her major effort and be unable to improve on — or even duplicate — that time during the remainder of the season. Physiologically, however, she is able to hold her racing form for five to eight weeks, during which she should be capable of five to eight peak performances at distances for which she has trained.

Often it is even possible to stretch your physical limits a little and run good times at longer distances than you are fully trained for. Thus, once he has reached his peak, a miler might squeeze a good 10K out of his mile training, or in an extreme case, a runner in peak 10K form might race a good half-marathon. Nearly always, however, these overdistance races will spell the end of that racing period, and the runner will need to return to base training and set his sights on races several weeks or months down the road.

Suppose, however, that you hit your time goal early in the season and don't want to move up to longer distances. In that case we recommend that you repeat the next-to-last and the last week of the schedule that led to your achieved goal. These two weeks of training may be repeated for as long as the season lasts — provided you remain eager to work and the training and racing results are satisfactory.

However, should you begin repeating the final two weeks of training after reaching a selected time goal and then find yourself floating through the workouts with too much ease, begin training for the next-fastest target time. Pick up that schedule in the fifth week and follow it until the end of your competitive season.

If, on the other hand, you are flat after your peak effort, it might be beneficial to move back to a slower target time. This helps you in two ways:

· You have time to recover physically and psychologically during the easier training
· Pride soon demands that you drop the easier schedule and move back to what has become your normal level

Once you feel that you have recovered, resume your original target schedule at the beginning of the fifth week.

## Benchmark Workouts

Often, the runner's problem is not what to do when he achieves his goals, but what to do when he thinks he's likely to fall short. As a general rule, if you have run the workouts leading up to your race, you will be able to run the time you have trained for. Physically, you are prepared. Often, however, runners can begin to *feel* unprepared, and workouts must be arranged to alleviate this mental sense of unreadiness. That is the purpose of the benchmark workout included in many of the schedules — a hard physical test that will prove to you that you're ready.

In 1973, one of my athletes, Len Hilton, slowly began to lose form several weeks before the U.S. National Championships. Although he had started the season well, a series of upper respiratory problems and lingering Achilles tendinitis had hurt his racing, and by late May he was almost convinced that his season was over. I, however, be-

*Leonard Hilton. (Photograph courtesy* Track and Field News)

lieved that he still had an untapped reserve of strength and power, built up over the preceding six months' training. My problem was how to restore Len's confidence before the rapidly approaching championship.

Ten days before the national mile heats, I asked Len to try one last workout before canceling the remainder of his track season. I made sure that the training days before this workout were easy and relaxed, so he would be at full strength for his effort.

The workout I had chosen was one that we had used before to assess Len's form: 6 × 500 meters, with only a 100-meter recovery jog. We knew that if Len could stay close to 60 seconds for the quarter-mile split, he was in top shape and in sub-4-minute-mile condition.

As Len progressed through his workout, I could see his confidence growing. Each time he flashed by the 400-meter mark, I would call out his time and yell, "Successful training means successful racing, Skinny!" By the time he began his fourth 500 he was smiling; by the time he began his sixth 500, he was shouting how easily he could have handled me if he had been running in my day. His 400-meter splits during his 500s were 58.5, 56.0, 59.0, 57.0, 60.0, and 58.5. After he completed the set he jogged a mile, then jauntily ran an 800 in 1:56 to show that he still had something left.

Eight days later he won his heat at the nationals in 4:00.5, and two days after that he outsprinted Marty Liquori to win the final — and the U.S. Mile Championship — in 3:55.9.

Experienced racers often use such benchmark workouts to find out where they are in their training and preparation. For runners who have already achieved their peak levels in earlier seasons, a benchmark workout can be a repeat of a solid interval series that they run season after season to confirm their readiness to race. When I was an international-level specialist at 5,000 and 10,000 meters, I would check my race preparation by running 4 × 1 mile at 4:30 with a 440 recovery. When I could complete that workout, I knew that I was in the same shape as when I had been successful in earlier international competitions.

I recall Rod Dixon, the great New Zealand runner, telling me that he had had a serious falling-off in form before the 1972 Munich Olympics. Despondent, he called his brother (also a top-class athlete) in New Zealand, who suggested that Rod try one of his favorite tough workouts before giving up on the European season. The workout Rod chose consisted of running as many laps as possible, with the first 200 meters run in 30 seconds, and the second 200 a "recovery" in 36 seconds. Rod completed almost 3 miles, passing through 2 miles in 8:42, before he was convinced that his strength and speed were at Olympic levels. Three weeks later he won the bronze medal in the 1,500-meter run.

The benchmark workout is even more important when a runner is attempting to break new ground, to run a PR (personal record), for example, or even to set a world record. In this instance, the workout provides, in addition to a gauge of physical ability, a strong psychological lift — "If I can run that workout, I can do anything!" Len Hilton's workout before the national championship is an example of this type.

But of course while Len's 3:55 was a world-class time, it was not a world record; people had run that fast before. When the psychological barriers are extremely great, correspondingly great benchmark workouts are needed. Thus in 1954 Roger Bannister felt he needed to be capable of running three-quarters of a mile in less than 3 minutes *in a workout* before he was ready to attempt the world's first 4-minute mile. Then he was ready, physically and mentally. In any case, the principle is the same — for Hilton, for Dixon, for Bannister, and for you: Successful training means successful racing.

## Competitive Track Racing

One difference I have often noted among American runners (especially distance runners) is their occasional inability to look out for themselves in major track competition, particularly when it involves some of the rough-and-tumble contact often characteristic of international track races.

I do not see Americans having such trouble in road races or in international cross-country competition, but track racing is unique because the only way to run an accurate race distance is to run close to the inside border of the track ("the pole"). The runner who cannot establish position on the pole is forced to race wide and therefore cover extra distance. On the other hand, a runner next to the curb is in danger of being "boxed in" — a feared condition in which a runner is trapped by runners ahead and to his side. Once in a box, a

*Contact was, and is, an integral part of the European circuit. Here 1956 Olympic silver medalist Gordon Pirie (second from right) shoulders his way through a narrow opening during a 5,000-meter race in Stockholm, 1957. (Photograph by Gert Zaar)*

runner cannot run his own race; he must either wait for the box to break up as his competitors fall off the pace; slow down himself and drop out of the back of the box (then try to catch up); or force his way out the side or the front, risking disqualification.

As bad as are the realities of being boxed, the psychological effects are usually much worse. Many track runners fear a box so much that they panic when they happen into one and don't wait to give it a chance to dissolve. Even if they avoid a drastic alteration of their race strategy, the psychological impact of their predicament causes them to spend energy worrying and give up prematurely on their race.

The way to avoid this problem in your racing is to train for it. At least once a week, organize a track workout with two to five of your training buddies. Let's say, for example, that you have planned a session of 20 quarters in 75 seconds. Since this is a relatively stiff workout, not all your friends will be running all of it; some may run 10 or 12 quarters with the group, some may run only the first 200 meters of each interval. In any case, you can use the workout as both a physical and a mental exercise by making it into a competitive game: Take turns seeing who can pace the group the closest to 75 seconds, changing positions after every effort. In such a workout you gain experience in pace judgment while leading, running half a lane wide, being caught in a box and — in general — getting thoroughly comfortable with close-quarters running.

Even front-runners need this sort of workout, because they too are going to find themselves in a crowd in major races. Without practice handling these types of situations, the results can be disastrous — as evidenced by the unfortunate Decker-Budd incident in the 1984 Olympic 3,000-meter final.

The skill of running in a crowd, like most skills discussed in this chapter, is unique to track racing, and must be practiced in your training on the track. Specific training information for the various track distances begins in the next chapter.

*Carl Lewis (387) versus Calvin Smith (711), 100-meter world-record holder, in the 1984 Olympic Trials. (Photograph by Jeff Johnson; courtesy* Track and Field News)

# THREE

# *100 Meters —*
# *200 Meters — 400 Meters*

SPRINTERS TEND TO THINK OF themselves as the thoroughbreds of track and field, and there is a special excitement and glamour associated with an individual who is labeled the World's Fastest Human — a title that can make the comparable rankings of King of the Roads for the best road racer and Chairman of the Boards for the best indoor runner seem like empty media hype. After all, running fast is what it's all about, isn't it? This sprinting mystique attracts many beginning runners who make a connection between speed and super athletic ability.

Often the sprinter's belief in the superiority of his event is matched by an equal belief in his own superiority; most elite sprinters have almost unlimited faith in their own ability. This confidence is often a result of having paid some "serious dues," as sprint specialist Boots Garland puts it, but — equally important — a sprinter has to have it to be successful.

Modern timing techniques are accurate to within 1/100th of a second, and races can be won or lost by a fraction of an inch. The slightest error in technique or a momentary loss of concentration can mean the difference between first place and several places back. It is this "close to the edge" existence that leads sprinters to develop a confidence which may well appear to other runners to be cockiness or arrogance. But it is often a necessary part of the elite sprinter's "race head"; in the sprints, more than in any other event, if you don't believe you will win, you won't.

Historically, the United States has produced a disproportionate number of medal winners in the Olympic sprint events (100 meters, 200 meters, 400 meters). Of the ninety medals awarded in these events between 1948 and 1984, U.S. sprinters have accounted for forty-five (eighteen gold, sixteen silver, eleven bronze). The number would undoubtedly be higher had the United States not boycotted the 1980 Games.

This supremacy has several possible causes. After discarding the most unlikely suggestions — that the competitive climate is better here or that the United States may have genetically superior sprinters (unlikely since America is populated entirely with people whose ancestors came from somewhere else in the world) — two possibilities remain.

- U.S. coaching knowledge in the sprints is more advanced
- Non-U.S. sprinters lack confidence when they run against Americans

It seems likely that both of these causes are important, since a large percentage of the non-U.S. medal winners have been products of the American intercollegiate system and have run against American sprinters often enough to know they can be beaten.

Successful sprinters are generally those runners with less than 30 percent slow-twitch fibers. But a high percentage of fast-twitch fibers does not guarantee that you will be a good sprinter — it merely gives you the tools to be one. Whether you do the work necessary to capitalize on your abilities is up to you. It is entirely possible that a potentially great sprinter with poor form, poor psychological preparation, or a poor start can be beaten by a sprinter with less talent who has minimized his deficiencies.

## The Start

Because all sprint races take less than a minute to complete, and the margin of victory is often so small, the sprints may well be the most psychological of all races. Therefore, a great deal of emphasis is often put on a good start — that is, one that helps you get the jump on the other sprinters in the same way that a gunfighter gets the drop on the other guy. Then, the reasoning goes, the other sprinters have to run to catch up.

How to get a good start has been, logically, a primary topic of discussion among sprint coaches and sprinters since the sport began. For toeholds, runners in the ancient Olympics could use grooves cut into the blocks marking the starting line, but sprinters in the first part of this century usually dug starting holes in the track to put their feet into. In 1929 American sprinter George Simpson recorded a blistering 9.4-second clocking for 100 yards, but his mark was not sanctioned by the International Amateur Athletic Federation because his starting blocks were considered an "artificial aid." When starting blocks were declared legal in 1948, the rate of record breaking increased rapidly.

On the other hand, some authorities maintain that a sprinter can start just as quickly from a standing position, and there is some evidence that supports this view. The only world-class runner who routinely used this iconoclastic technique was Allan Wells, a Scots sprinter who won the gold medal in the 100 meters in the 1980 Moscow Olympics and took the silver in the 200 meters behind world-record holder Pietro Mennea of Italy. Ironically, Wells was not allowed to race from a standing start — modern timing equipment uses an athlete's foot pressure on the starting blocks to judge false starts. Thus blocks, once an illegal aid, have now become a requirement.

Once blocks became the norm, the next question addressed was how far behind the front block the rear one should be ("pad spacing," in the idiom of the sport). As the debate evolved, the choices resolved into three:

- the ELONGATED start, in which the distance between the feet is 21 to 26 inches
- the MEDIUM start, spacing 14 to 18 inches
- the BUNCH, or BULLET, start, spacing 11 to 12 inches

The elongated start enjoyed its greatest popularity in the early twentieth century, when coaching knowledge favored an almost straight rear leg. By the mid-twenties, research seemed to show that the bunch start produced the quickest block clearance, and most elite athletes adopted this form.

By the mid-fifties it was clear that much of the early research conclusions were incorrect. While the bunch start *does* allow quicker block clearance, the athlete leaves the blocks at a slower rate of acceleration and thus is at a disadvantage over the full length of the race. The ideal block placement is one that takes full advantage of the laws of physics and allows a sprinter to reach maximum speed at the optimum point in the race.

The starting position described below, which Olympic Track Coach Tom Tellez has used to develop world-class sprinters such as Carl Lewis and Kirk Baptiste, has one apparent disadvantage: It slightly increases a runner's block-clearance time, so that his start is not quite so instantaneous as with the bullet start. As we will see later, however, that is only an *apparent* disadvantage.

## HAND AND UPPER-BODY PLACEMENT

Both hands should be spread just behind the starting line, fingers loosely together and pointing out, thumbs pointing in. They should be shoulder-width apart, and your shoulders should be directly above them when you are in your starting stance, so that your arms are straight and perpendicular to the ground and your center of gravity is as high as it can be. In the starting position, your back will be straight and make a slight slope upward from your shoulders toward your hips, and your head should be directly in line with your back. You will thus be looking down at the track a few inches behind your hands, not at the finish line. (Looking toward the finish, as some coaches recommend, will almost always force you to lower your hips as you leave the blocks, and cost you time and energy as you raise them back up into normal running posture.)

## BLOCK AND FOOT PLACEMENT

Every sprinter should spend enough time starting out in blocks to feel comfortable, but at first it will seem to be a very awkward position, one that may pitch you facedown on the track as soon as you move forward.

For nearly every runner, the front block should be set so that the toes of the front foot are approximately 13 inches behind the starting line. From this position, refine your block placement so that your front leg (the "weaker" leg, which for most runners is the left leg) will make a 90-degree angle at the knee and your back leg will make an angle of between 130 and 135 degrees when you are "set." (One way to check this is to have a training buddy take a quick-developing photo of your starting stance and then measure the photo with a small protractor).

The toes of your back foot will be set on the block face — that is, the metal of the spikes will rest on the block itself. The back foot's job is to provide a quick stretch-reflex impulse straight forward and to start the body moving forward for the front leg to take over. Your front foot, however, should be set so that the spikes are on the track and the shoe sole under your arch touches the block. This enables you to use the entire extension of your calf muscles in the front-leg drive out of the blocks, providing maximum drive off the block rather than quick clearance.

*SPRINTING ACTION*

After the runner is off the blocks, most of the information written on sprint form can be reduced to two basic rules:

- Any inefficiency will cost you time. Think of trying to keep all the movements of any body part in a straight line toward the finish.
- In the words of Boots Garland, "Stand *up* and run." Once the initial impulse from the blocks has impelled you to speed, any forward lean is inefficient because it shortens your stride length, and it forces your body to use nonrunning muscles to hold it up. You can check this for yourself by leaning forward as you run: You'll feel tension along your back and the backs of your thighs as those muscles work to keep you upright; your toes will probably dig slightly into the running surface as they touch down before your legs reach full extension.

The other area of leg form that requires attention is the amount of "whip" a sprinter has in the trail leg as it leaves the ground and bends at the knee. Runners who have trained on the roads may have too little follow-through because distance running requires less leg action for maximum efficiency. On the other hand, because a sprinter concentrates on speed and speed is a function of stride frequency, there can be a tendency to rush the trail leg, to try to get it out in front of you faster than it wants to go. Rushing this action will only slow you down, because, according to the laws of physics, when you allow the leg to carry through its normal swing and bring the heel close to the buttock, the "effective lever," which is a function of leg length, is much shorter and can be moved more quickly. Moving the leg forward too soon not only hurries the stride but asks the body to move the leg at almost full extension, a harder and a slower task. (The principle of physics involved here is the same that lets skaters and gymnasts spin faster when they bring their arms in closer to their bodies. You can check it for yourself by moving your arm up and down fully extended, then bent at the elbow with your hand on your shoulder.)

One additional area of form needs to be addressed, especially for those sprinters who began their running careers on the roads: *arm swing.* Here is the chance to use all that strength you acquired in your weight training. Slow-motion studies of sprinters in action reveal that the forward arm movement during sprinting not only balances the thrust of the opposite leg but actually initiates the stride and "pops" the runner forward as well.

Many road-trained runners make the mistake of simply swinging their arms harder when they're sprinting, without changing their style. But in typical road-running style, the hands move toward the centerline of the body as they come forward and the elbows move forward and back from the area of the hipbone.

In sprinting, both these movements are errors. Good arm swing in sprinting keeps the hands moving almost straight forward from the sides, with very little movement toward the centerline. If you have done a lot of road training, this movement will feel awkward to you, as though you are being jerked forward alternately by one shoulder, then the other. Ideally, your hands should never go behind the centerline of your body (or your hipbone, for easy reference); in front, your hands should come up until they're even with your eyes. In essence, then, a good sprinting arm swing takes place almost *all in front* of the body; but if you try it while jogging, it can be one of the most awkward feelings you will ever experience in running. When you use it while sprinting, however, you can actually feel it pull you forward; the sense of awkwardness is replaced by a sense of the power of the action. The only limiting factor is that it is tiring and so is practical only for the short distances involved in sprint racing — and after all, that's why you did all that weight training.

Sprint coaches have different mnemonics to help their runners remember to keep their hands high in the sprints. Some say to watch for your hands in front of your face; others find it more effective to talk about keeping the *elbows* up. For a finishing touch, you might want to extend your hands like spears à la Carl Lewis, but that looks a bit presumptuous unless you also have his speed. He does that, by the way, not to streamline his body, as some track writers have guessed, but because it helps him remember to "stroke" each stride; power is more efficient when delivered smoothly.

## A Word About Intelligence

Once you have learned the fundamentals of sprint technique and have gotten a comfortable position to start from, you may feel that the rest is just a matter of finding out who's the fastest. Sprinting is often thought of as being the most physical and least mental of all races. After all, there aren't any tactics — you can't outthink one of your competitors; you never hear of a sprinter's running a "smart" race.

In some ways, however, the sprints may be the most purely intellectual of all races, because instead of outsmarting some other runner to run well, you need to understand and take advantage of the laws of physics.

Nowhere is that approach to sprinting more evident than in the coaching philosophy of Tom Tellez. Tellez believes that the start should initiate a pattern of acceleration that allows a runner to cover the *entire race distance* most quickly, not just the first 10 or 20 yards.

Tellez's philosophy is innovative and successful. It is based on the long-recognized concept that a runner cannot accelerate for the full length of the 100-meter race. Most runners will begin to slow between 50 and 60 meters. After that point, the runner who *runs the fastest* will be the one who *decelerates the least*. Awareness of this fact has led sprint coaches to emphasize (1) relaxation over the last

50 yards (on the principle that the runner who is "fighting his body" will slow down more) and (2) weight training (on the principle that a stronger runner will be able to maintain acceleration longer).

Tellez believes that a quick start leads to a rapid acceleration through the early stages of a 100-meter sprint race. Thus a quick starter may gain a yard or two over a slower starter and may actually increase that lead up to halfway through the race. Then, however, he will inevitably begin to decelerate while a slower starter may still be accelerating. Finally, when the slower starter reaches peak velocity at 60 to 70 meters and begins *his* inevitable deceleration, he will slow for the last 30 to 40 meters instead of the last 50. This final improvement may not seem like much, but in an event where wins and losses are measured in hundredths of a second, an advantage of 20 percent in one phase of the race may be overwhelmingly decisive.

For a sprinter to be successful with this biomechanically superior approach is not an easy task, because it requires that he be intelligent enough to understand it and that he believe in it so strongly that he can tolerate being *behind* in the early stages of the race. If he works to catch up, even unconsciously, he will alter his acceleration pattern and thus damage his chances of winning the race over the last 40 meters. It is the ability of Carl Lewis and Kirk Baptiste to run their own races that sets them apart from many of the world's other fine sprinters. Baptiste is especially interesting because he is a converted 400-meter runner who has been able to accept Tellez's coaching philosophy and become a world-class short-distance sprinter as a result.

## Phases of the Sprint

To review, to sum up, and to incorporate all the elements of the winning philosophy in one place, it is possible to break a sprint race into phases. This step helps a sprinter in training to organize his race into manageable sections, but you should never forget, of course, that each section grows out of the last and is the foundation of the next and that the great sprinters are unified and smooth.

"On your marks!": Hands behind the starting line, front foot in the block with the toes well onto the track surface, back foot in the block with the tip of the toe just touching the track surface. Knee of

*Coach Tom Tellez watches two of his sprinters practice the three phases of the start. (Photograph by Robert S. Cozens)*

the back leg on the track surface, supporting some of your body weight. Eyes look down at the track in the area of the starting line.

"Set!": Keeping hands and feet in place on the track, raise your body as high as possible. Your body will displace slightly forward and will now slope downward from the hips toward the shoulders, so that if your head stays in proper body alignment, your eyes now look at the track between the starting line and the front block. Your feet are in the "normal" 90-degree angle to your calves. You should feel pressure on the soles of your feet in both blocks, and you should not feel that you are holding yourself up with your arms alone.

"Gun!": Sprinters are often told to concentrate on the gun. This advice frequently leads them to lose time after they have identified the gun sound. It is more productive for you to concentrate on the first action of your sprint; you will certainly hear the gun without listening for it. The sprinter should therefore think of the first step, which is taken with the leg in the back block. (The drive of that leg off its block is a stretch reflex, so it doesn't need to be concentrated on.) You should come off the front block at a 45-degree angle to the ground, with your head, shoulders, and hips in a straight line. (Coaches often suggest, mistakenly, that sprinters should keep their heads and shoulders low; this, however, shortens the stride and throws the runner off balance.)

*First Phase.* As you leave the blocks, you establish a pattern of acceleration in which each step is slightly longer and slightly quicker than the one preceding. Concentrate on keeping this acceleration smooth and consistent to the point of maximum speed, which you should reach between 60 and 70 meters in a 100-meter dash.

*Second Phase.* As you reach maximum speed, any attempt to continue accelerating will merely slow you down more quickly. As soon as this point is reached, concentrate on *relaxing* and *maintaining.* Efficient use of this technique, with awareness of exactly when to use it, will result in no speed loss for 20 to 25 meters.

*Third Phase.* Over the last 10 to 15 meters in a 100-meter dash, you are going to slow down. Any attempts to increase speed, to "muscle" or "hammer" through the last yards, will only slow you down faster. Here you should concentrate on *relaxation* and *smoothness.* Here is where, in many cases, the race is won or lost. Often, as many coaches say, it is not who runs the fastest who wins the race, but rather who slows down the least.

## The Finish

Sprint races traditionally conclude with a dramatic lean into the tape, as one runner tries to hurl his body across the line just before his competition does. It is undoubtedly true that a forward dip at just the right time can cut a fraction of a second off your sprint time. But it is also true that many more races — and places — have been lost through mistimed leans than won through leans made at just the right time.

If you look at a number of close sprint finishes, you will note that runners executing the lean seem to be susceptible to the "herd ef-

*Former world-record holder and three-time Olympic gold medalist Jim Hines (closest to the pole, gray singlet) dips here at the right moment; everyone else leans too soon. (Photograph from archives of Texas Striders Athletic Club; courtesy David Rickey)*

fect." The leading runner dips at the right time, and all those competing with him dip in the hopes of edging him out. In many cases, however, the competing runners may be several yards back when they lean for the tape, and thus they may have jeopardized their chances at third or fourth place by cutting their last strides short.

The old track adage "Run *through* the tape" is the best advice to follow in planning your sprint finish. Run your own race. Your body will instinctively dip at the right time.

## The Curves

There is a mystique associated with curve running that may or may not have much to do with the reality of the sprinting situation. When a sprinter can run a world-class 100-meter time and only a fair time for the 200 meters, it is common to hear that he can't run the curves. The implication is that a good curve-runner has a special form or mental attitude that allows him to suffer less from the centrifugal force generated by running fast in a tight semicircle.

The realities of curve running are more easily assessed. First, the inside lane has a much tighter curve than the outside lane. (It has been estimated that runners in Lane 1 run between 0.050 and 0.075 of a second slower per curve than those in the far outside lane.) Many sprinters find drawing an inside lane more psychological pressure than they can handle, while others make the best of it by claiming that they have an advantage because they can see all their competitors for most of the race.

A second important element is physiological. There are two different power-producing mechanisms at work in the sprints. So in many cases what appears to be "inability to handle the curves" may in fact be lack of conditioning for the event.

Finally, we come to the reality of physics. As a sprinter's body accelerates around a curve, inertia tends to push it straight ahead and thus to the outside. To counteract this force, sprinters have sometimes been told to (1) lower the inside, or left, arm, (2) drive the outside arm powerfully across the body, or (3) lean into the curve or turn the right shoulder and upper body across the lane toward the inside.

Tellez maintains that these measures (except for a slight sideways

*Kirk Baptiste running the curve for a silver medal in the 1984 Olympic 200 meters. (Photograph by Cor Eberhard; courtesy* Track and Field News)

lean) make no biomechanical sense. A runner will automatically make the necessary adjustments to stay within his lane without thinking about it. So, Tellez reasons, you should concentrate on your acceleration pattern and on maintaining the best possible form within the constraints that your body automatically supplies as you run the curve. Your 200-meter acceleration pattern should allow you to accelerate off the curve, so in effect you need to slow your initial rate of acceleration and reach peak speed 120 to 130 meters into the race.

One exception to the rule of making no changes when running the curves: Block placement in both the 200-meter and 400-meter events should allow the first step or two to be in a straight line. This means that the blocks will be placed as close as possible to the outside line but pointing toward the inside line several yards down the curve. A sketch may make this easier to understand:

As the arrow shows, the sprinter will almost clip the inside lane marker, coming out of the blocks in a straight line for the first critical yards before settling into her acceleration pattern around the curve.

## Relays

At some point in your sprinting career, you may want to participate in relay competition with your teammates. While nearly everything written in this chapter also applies to running relays, there is one crucial addition: the exchange.

Technically speaking, "the exchange" applies only to the moment in which the baton is passed from one runner to the next. A well-handled exchange literally cuts meters off the distance the team has to run, since trained runners often can extend a baton to a runner two strides ahead. Because of the timing necessary, the relay exchange requires more practice than any other area of sprinting competition — except the start.

The first requirement in timing is that both runners be running at peak speed when the exchange occurs. If the receiving runner waits too long to start his acceleration as his teammate is approaching, he will be "run up on" and perhaps bumped. (If the baton is dropped during this transfer, only the runner who dropped it may pick it up.) Even if the exchange does take place, the receiving runner then has to accelerate to sprint speed. Such a problem is called a dead-stick exchange, probably with reference to the fact that in a well-handled transfer the baton seems to jump ahead several yards.

Relay runners avoid dead-stick exchanges by careful practice to determine when the receiving runner should begin his sprint acceleration. Through trial and error, the team finds the point at which an incoming runner will be at the optimum moment and (traditionally) puts a bit of adhesive tape on the track at that spot. The waiting runner gets into a sprinting crouch, feet pointing the way he will be going, and twists his body slightly to the inside to watch his teammate's approach. When the incoming runner crosses the tape, the receiving runner sprints forward without looking behind and listens for the command "Stick!" which tells him that the incoming runner is close enough to make the exchange. The actual exchange may be one of two different types: visual or blind.

The visual exchange is the easiest to master. When the incoming runner gives the command "Stick!" the receiving runner turns back in full stride, focuses on the extended baton in the incoming run-

*A good visual exchange advances the baton several yards. (Photograph by Conrad J. McCarthy)*

ner's hand, and takes it. Usually this will be a right-hand-to-left-hand exchange, to minimize dropped batons, but there are a number of sophisticated variations worked out by coaches to cut a few hundredths of a second off the time. (Incoming runners should remember to hold the baton by the bottom third, so there will be enough room for the receiving runner to get a grip.) The visual exchange is used in the longer sprint distances, such as the 4 × 400-meter relay, the distance medley, and beyond.

The blind exchange is faster but requires perfect timing to avoid a dropped baton or lost seconds. In this exchange, the receiving runner does not look back but simply extends his arm backward, hand open and slightly cupped, palm up. The incoming runner pops the baton into the open hand with enough force that the receiving runner knows he's got it; he closes his hand around it and continues his sprint acceleration, scarcely having altered his running action while taking the baton. When four runners are involved, the baton exchange usually is executed left-to-right-to-left-to-right. When well done, not only fast but beautiful, the blind exchange is used in events that may be won or lost by fractions of a second, notably the 4 × 100-meter relay and the sprint medley.

## Sprint Training

Once you know what will be required of you in a sprint race, your sprint training is easier to figure out. Good sprint training includes elements of weight training and flexibility, of course, but obviously the single most important training you can do is to practice running sprints.

That does *not* mean that you need to go to the track, put on your spikes, and run 4 × 100 meters as fast as you can. Good sprint training can be divided into the trainable elements of the sprint itself. A good sprinter needs three things: rapid turnover, strength, and specific training.

Rapid turnover is in part a function of fast-twitch fibers, and that, naturally, to some extent is fixed. You can also decrease your stride frequency by failing to follow through with your stride, so make sure in your training runs that your heel rises toward your buttocks as you move your leg forward. The simple fact that you have long legs will decrease your turnover rate, but in theory that weakness will be overcome by your innate tendency to have a longer stride length.

Stride length will also vary according to strength; if you're stronger, each stride will propel you farther down the track. You should be careful not to overstride, however: If your foot lands too far ahead, you will be putting on the brakes instead of increasing your speed. All running is *pushing,* not pulling.

Specific training for sprints concentrates on building anaerobic endurance by including both short, quick-turnover power sprints (up to 80 meters) and longer-distance "slow" sprints (up to 800 meters) in your workouts. In all training, you should endeavor to use the same running form, acceleration patterns, and maintenance phases you will use in the race; this ensures that your training will be as effective as possible. Any deviation from race conditions will result in training other muscle groups that won't be used.

But of course you will *not* be running all your sprints at the same speed as you hope to run in a race — if you tried, you should logically be able to produce only one repeat 100 or 200 per workout. Sprinters who are coached in college or on national teams often have their workouts drawn up in a kind of coaching shorthand. They may be told to do 6 × 150 meters at seven-eighths effort or 4 × 200 at 90 percent.

These figures will mean little to the self-coached sprinter who is a novice in the short events. What exactly is seven-eighths or three-quarters effort? How fast is 90 percent? Most college runners have learned what those figures mean through a process of trial and error, beginning in their early years of being coached. After several years of being yelled at to "Pick it up!" if the coach thought they were giving less effort than he asked for, and of being cautioned to "Take it easy!" if the coach thought they were running too fast, almost anyone could have arrived at a sense of pace to fit those phrases — but almost no runner could explain what they mean in objective terms.

In the following schedules, we have tried to make it easier for the novice sprinter to determine how fast he should be running in his training. These schedules should be interpreted by the self-coached runner in light of specific needs and specific goals. They are designed for sprinters who plan some indoor competition in January and February and a full outdoor season in the spring; if you plan to skip the indoor season entirely, you will want to replace some of the more intense "sharpening" workouts before indoor season with workouts that will bring you along more slowly.

No matter during which seasons you plan to race, some basic training principles need to be set out before specific training begins, to remind you that sprinting requires a disciplined and structured approach. A sprinter must place importance on several areas of body development, including:

- strength — through a comprehensive weight program to strengthen major muscle groups and the upper body
- flexibility — by stretching the crucial muscle groups used in sprinting
- technique sessions — practicing starts and running-style bio-mechanics
- running training — actual on-track workouts, which are the single most important part of sprint training

With regard to this last element, there are also a number of *do*'s and *don't*'s a sprinter should keep in mind:

- DO low-intensity work in your training, especially at first
- DO concentrate on relaxation at all times while running
- DO concentrate on correct biomechanical movement while running
- DO include resistance running (hills, stadium steps, or parking ramps) during the first ten weeks of pre-competitive conditioning
- DO master correct pace judgment in longer (200- to 800-meter) training runs (i.e., try to run each 100-meter section at the same pace — neither "fire out and burn out" nor "sit and kick")
- DO replace quantity with quality as the season progresses
- DON'T race in training
- DON'T fall apart and lose form by running too hard in training
- DON'T be afraid to hold back to make sure that you maintain good relaxation and biomechanical movements

The ONLY exception to these rules comes after the first ten weeks of conditioning, when the starting practices should begin to increase gradually in intensity, until, when the season begins, the sprinter is coming off the blocks in a full simulation of race conditions for 20 or 30 yards.

# Sprint Training Schedule

In this typical schedule, designed for some indoor competition with an emphasis on spring outdoor racing, "R" means recovery. Recovery should be jogged unless otherwise stated. Distances are given in meters. On a nonmetric track, 220 yards is very close to 200 meters, 440 yards equals about 400 meters, and so on.

**September** (a one-week program that should be repeated until the month is over)

| | |
|---|---|
| *Monday* | Weight training (check specific program in Chapter 2) |
| *Tuesday* | 45:00 cross-country running incorporating 15:00 fartlek training (see Glossary) |
| *Wednesday* | Weight training |
| *Thursday* | 45:00 cross-country incorporating 10:00 uphill running |
| *Friday* | Weight training |
| *Saturday* | 10 × 100 (best 100 + 1.5 seconds); 100 walk R |
| *Sunday* | Rest day |

Repeat this program for the entire month

**October** (a two-week cycle that should be repeated once)

| | |
|---|---|
| *Monday* | Weight training |
| *Tuesday* | 45:00 cross-country incorporating 15:00 fartlek training |
| *Wednesday* | Weight training |
| *Thursday* | 6 × 200 (best 200 + 4 seconds); 400 walk R |
| *Friday* | Weight training |
| *Saturday* | • 1 × 600 (best 200 + 10–14 seconds, multiplied × 3); 6:00–8:00 rest |
| | • 1 × 300 (best 100 + 4–6 seconds, multiplied × 3); 6:00–8:00 rest |
| | • 1 × 200 (best 200 + 3–6 seconds) |
| *Sunday* | Rest day |
| *Monday* | Weight training |
| *Tuesday* | 45:00 cross-country incorporating 15:00 uphill running |
| *Wednesday* | Weight training |
| *Thursday* | 8–12 × 100 (best 100 + 1–2 seconds); 100 walk R |
| *Friday* | 45:00 easy cross-country running |
| *Saturday* | • 1 × 500 (best 200 + 8–12 seconds, multiplied × 2.5); 400 walk R |

- 1 × 400 (best 200 + 5–7 seconds, multiplied × 2); 400 walk R
- 1 × 200 (best 200 + 3–5 seconds)

*Sunday*      Rest day

Repeat for the remainder of October

## November

### Week 1

*Monday*      10 × 100 (best 100 + 1–2 seconds); 100 walk R
*Tuesday*     Weight training
*Wednesday*   • 4–6 acceleration drills through the curves, each drill to consist of 30 meters easy, 70 meters rapid acceleration, 20 meters easy
              • 6–10 easy gun starts, concentrating on starting technique and smooth acceleration
*Thursday*    3 × 300 (best 100 + 2–3 seconds, multiplied × 3); 400 walk R
*Friday*      Weight training
*Saturday*    Rest day
*Sunday*      Rest day

### Week 2

*Monday*      8 × 200 (best 200 + 3–5 seconds)
*Tuesday*     Weight training
*Wednesday*   • 5 easy gun starts, running out for 20 meters
              • 3 gun starts at race pace for 35 meters
              • 4 acceleration drills of 75 yards, beginning on curve
*Thursday*    • 1 × 400 (best 200 + 5 seconds, multiplied × 2); 5:00–6:00 R
              • 1 × 300 meters (best 100 + 2.5–3 seconds, multiplied × 3)
*Friday*      Weight training
*Saturday*    30:00 easy cross-country running
*Sunday*      Rest day

### Week 3

*Monday*      2 × 600 (best 200 + 9–12 seconds, multiplied × 3); 5:00 rest
*Tuesday*     Weight training
*Wednesday*   • 6–8 fast starts, concentrating on technique
              • 6–8 times up ramp or stadium steps
*Thursday*    10 × 100 (best 100 + 1–2 seconds); 220 walk R
*Friday*      Weight training
*Saturday*    30:00 easy cross-country running
*Sunday*      Rest day

### Week 4

Repeat any of the first three weeks

## December
### Week 1

| | |
|---|---|
| *Monday* | 2–3 × 400 (best 200 + 5 seconds, multiplied × 2); 200 walk *or* 400 jog R |
| *Tuesday* | Weight training |
| *Wednesday* | • 6–8 starts, 35 meters, concentrating on technique |
| | • 2–3 × 150, concentrating on acceleration (last 100 at best 100 + 0.5 second) |
| *Thursday* | Weight training |
| *Friday* | 6–10 × 100 with a running start (best 100 + 1 second) |
| *Saturday* | Rest day |
| *Sunday* | Rest day |

### Week 2

| | |
|---|---|
| *Monday* | • 1 × 500 (best 200 + 6–8 seconds, multiplied × 2.5); walk/jog 6:00 R |
| | • 1 × 400 (best 200 + 5–7 seconds, multiplied × 2); walk/jog 6:00 R |
| | • 1 × 300 (best 100 + 2 seconds, multiplied × 3) |
| *Tuesday* | Weight training |
| *Wednesday* | • 10:00 stadium steps or up ramps |
| | • 6–8 starts, 40 meters, for technique |
| | • 2–4 × 100 with running start (best 100 + 1 second) |
| *Thursday* | Weight training |
| *Friday* | *100/200 sprinters:* 6 × 100 (best 100 + 0.6 second); 200 walk R |
| | *400 sprinters:* 3 × 300 (best 100 + 1.5 seconds, multiplied × 3); 400 walk R |
| *Saturday* | Rest day |
| *Sunday* | Rest day |

### Week 3

| | |
|---|---|
| *Monday* | 4–6 × 200 (best 200 + 2–3 seconds); 400 walk R |
| *Tuesday* | Weight training |
| *Wednesday* | • 6–8 starts, 40 meters |
| | • 2 × 150, accelerating around half of curve (last 100 at best 100 + 1 second); 300 walk R |
| *Thursday* | Weight training |
| *Friday* | Rest day |
| *Saturday* | Practice meet |
| | *100/200 sprinters:* 1 effort at 60 meters; 15:00 R; 1 effort at 150 meters |
| | *400 sprinters:* 1 effort at 500 meters; 15:00 R; 1 effort at 150 meters |
| *Sunday* | Rest day |

### Week 4

| | |
|---|---|
| *Monday* | 5–8 × 100 (best 100 + 1 second); 200 walk R |
| *Tuesday* | Weight training |

| | |
|---|---|
| *Wednesday* | 6 starts over 40 meters, then: |
| | *100/200 sprinters:* 2 × 300 (best 100 + 1.5 seconds, multiplied × 3); 400 walk R |
| | *400 sprinters:* 2 × 500 (best 200 + 6 seconds, multiplied × 2.5); walk/jog 5:00 R |
| *Thursday* | Weight training |
| *Friday* | 45:00 cross-country with 10:00 hills |
| *Saturday* | Rest day |
| *Sunday* | Rest day |

## January

### Week 1

| | |
|---|---|
| *Monday* | *100/200 sprinters:* |
| | • 1 × 300 meters (best 100 + 1.5 seconds, multiplied × 3); 400 walk R |
| | • 1 × 200 (best 200 + 1.5 seconds); 400 walk R |
| | • 2 × 100 (best 100 + 0.6 second); 300 walk R |
| | *400 sprinters:* |
| | • 1 × 600 (best 200 + 6–8 seconds, multiplied × 3); 600 walk R |
| | • 1 × 500 (best 200 + 5–7 seconds, multiplied × 2.5); 600 walk R |
| | • 1 × 400 (best 400 + 4–6 seconds) |
| *Tuesday* | Weight training |
| *Wednesday* | • 6–8 starts, 45 meters |
| | • 4–8 × 75, concentrating on acceleration pattern and technique |
| *Thursday* | Weight training |
| *Friday* | Rest day |
| *Saturday* | Indoor competition *or* practice meet |
| | *100/200 sprinters:* |
| | • 1 × 60, maximum effort |
| | • 1 × 150, maximum effort |
| | *400 sprinters:* |
| | • 1 × 300, maximum effort |
| | • 1 × 150, maximum effort |
| *Sunday* | Rest day |

### Week 2

| | |
|---|---|
| *Monday* | 6 × 100 (best 100 + 1 second) |
| *Tuesday* | Weight training |
| *Wednesday* | • 4–6 starts, 45 meters; and |
| | *100–200 sprinters:* 4–6 × 150 acceleration drills; 300 walk R |
| | *400 sprinters:* 3–6 × 200 (best 200 + 2–4 seconds); 400 walk R |
| *Thursday* | Weight training (or rest day if competing on Saturday) |
| *Friday* | Rest day |
| *Saturday* | Competition *or* repeat practice meet from previous week |
| *Sunday* | Rest day |

At this point in the training cycle, training differs for those who will be competing in the indoor sprint season and those who are focusing primarily on the outdoor season.

**Indoor competitors:** For the next six weeks during the indoor competition season, competing sprinters should repeat the two-week January schedule, modifying it to fit racing dates. During the training phases of the indoor season, 100- and 200-meter sprinters should concentrate on starts, running technique, and perfection of acceleration patterns, while 400-meter sprinters should add race pace to this list.

**Outdoor competitors:** Sprinters who are training through the indoor season should follow this training maintenance program:

| | |
|---|---|
| *Monday* | 6–10 × 100 (best 100 + 1 second); 300 walk R |
| *Tuesday* | Weight training |
| *Wednesday* | • 6–8 starts, 40 meters; and |
| | *100/200 sprinters:* 2 × 150 accelerating around curve (last 100 at best 100 + 1 second); 300 walk R |
| | *400 sprinters:* 2–3 × 300 (best 100 + 1.5 seconds, multiplied × 3); 400 walk R |
| *Thursday* | Weight training |
| *Friday* | 45:00 cross-country running incorporating 15:00 hill running |
| *Saturday* | Rest day |
| *Sunday* | Rest day |

# Outdoor Season Training Schedule

By the time the outdoor competitive season begins, the sprinter who has been training and competing since the fall is in a perfect position to "springboard" into this important part of the competitive year. There is one important consideration that needs to be taken into account: Sprinters must take care of their legs in much the same way that a baseball pitcher needs to take care of his arm. Accordingly (in addition to weight work and flexibility drills), we recommend that sprinters wear tights in all practices to help prevent injuries; in colder areas of the United States, it might be advisable to wear track bottoms over the tights.

There should be a ten-day rest period after the conclusion of the

*Tights help prevent muscle injury during cold-weather workouts. (Photograph by Robert S. Cozens)*

indoor season. The first week of training after it should be devoted to bringing the body back to the same degree of conditioning and sharpness it had prior to the rest period.

### Week 1

| | |
|---|---|
| *Monday* | *100/200 sprinters:* |

• 6 × 100 (best 100 + 0.6–1 second); 220 walk R
• 2 × 150 from blocks (last 100 at best 100 + 0.5 second); walk 250 R
*400 sprinters:*
• 6 × 100 (best 100 + 0.6–1 second); 220 walk R
• 2 × 300 from blocks (best 100 + 1 second, multiplied × 3); 400 walk R

*Tuesday*  Weight training
*Wednesday*  4–6 × 50, sprint from blocks; walk back R
*100/200 sprinters:*
• 3 × 75, sprint from blocks; 2:00–3:00 R
• 2 × 200 (best 200 + 2–2.5 seconds) with running start, concentrating on acceleration pattern
*400 sprinters:*
• 1 × 600 (best 200 + 6 seconds, multiplied × 3); 10:00 rest
• 1 × 400 (best 400 + 3–4 seconds)

| | |
|---|---|
| *Thursday* | Weight training |
| *Friday* | 45:00 easy cross-country running |
| *Saturday* | 6 × 50, sprint from blocks; walk back R |
| | 3 × 150 from blocks, practicing accelerating through the turn; 250 walk R |
| *Sunday* | Rest day |

## Week 2

*Monday*  
*100/200 sprinters:*
- 8 × 100 with running start (best 100 + 0.5 second); 100 walk R

*400 sprinters:*
- 1 × 500 (best 200 + 4 seconds, multiplied × 2.5); 600 walk R
- 1 × 300 (best 100 + 1 second, multiplied × 3); 500 walk R
- 1 × 200 (best 200 + 2–3 seconds)

*Tuesday*  Weight training

*Wednesday*  4–8 × 45 from blocks; walk back R; and

*100/200 sprinters:*
- 2 × 150 from blocks, practicing acceleration through curve; 250 walk R
- 2 × 100 with running start (best 100 + 0.5 second); 100 walk R

*400 sprinters:*
- 2 × 300 (best 100 + 1 second, multiplied × 3); 400 walk R
- 1 × 200 (best 200 + 2 seconds)

*Thursday*  Weight training (but if sprinter is competing in an *important* meet on Saturday, Thursday should be a *rest day*)

*Friday*  Rest day

*Saturday*  Competition

*Sunday*  Rest day

An alternative outdoor training program for the competitive season would be:

*Monday*  
*100/200 sprinters:*
- 4 × 100 with running start (best 100 + 0.5 second); 100 walk R
- 4 × 75 from standing start, practicing acceleration pattern; 100 walk R
- 2 × 50 with running start around curve; 100 walk R

*400 sprinters:*
- 1 × 600 (best 200 + 6 seconds, multiplied × 3); 600 walk R
- 1 × 500 (best 200 + 4 seconds, multiplied × 3); 600 walk R
- 2 × 200 with running start (best 200 + 2.5 seconds); 400 walk R

*Tuesday*  Weight training

*Wednesday*   6–8 starts over 40 meters, and
*100/200 sprinters:*
- 2 × 75, sprint from blocks; walk back R
- 2 × 200 with running start (best 200 + 2 seconds); 400 walk R

*400 sprinters:*
- 1 × 400 (best 400 + 4 seconds); 400 walk R
- 1 × 300 (best 100 + 1 second, multiplied × 3); 400 walk R
- 1 × 200 (best 200 + 2 seconds)

*Thursday*   Rest day *or* 30:00 warming up and stretching
*Friday*   Rest day
*Saturday*   Competition

These schedules can be interchanged for the rest of the competitive season. Strength training (weights) should be modified before all important meets and late in the competitive season. Early in the sprinter's training, lifting should be done twice each week (Tuesday and Thursday), but before important competition it is recommended that the Thursday session be dropped. A general rule of thumb for tapering before a big meet is "The more important the meet, the more rest is required." This standard is strongly recommended by Tom Tellez and other top sprint coaches.

*Sebastian Coe, 800-meter world-record holder and Olympic 1,500-meter gold medalist, shown running his 1981 world-record mile (3:47.33). (Photograph by Theo van de Rakt; courtesy* Track and Field News*)*

# FOUR

# 800 Meters —
# 880 Yards — Half-Mile

IN THE LAST TWO DECADES, track racing has seen a number of changes in tactics and training philosophy, and the 800-meter/880-yard race has seen perhaps the greatest change: Not only has it been affected by the training modifications that have touched all distances, but the race itself has changed from a middle-distance run to an extended sprint.

In part as a result of this, the half-mile distance has been the site for a tremendous struggle between two very different types of runners: *the sprinters and the milers.* Sprinters running the half-mile distance are usually quarter-milers moving up; they are characterized by the typical sprinter build and a powerful upper body. When this powerful build is combined with the height necessary for efficient use of that power in the long strides of the quarter-mile, the result is a tall, powerful athlete. The best example of such a half-miler is Alberto Juantorena (six foot two, 175 pounds). Nicknamed *El Caballo* (The Horse) for his size and his powerful action, he dominated the half-mile distance in the early seventies, setting a world record and winning Olympic gold medals at Montreal in 1976 in the 400 and 800 meters. In contrast to this type is the slightly built miler moving down to the half-mile distance. Best typified in recent years by the British runner Sebastian Coe (five foot eight, 138 pounds), these athletes are only moderately tall and are much lighter than the sprinter.

Whether you are the sprinter type or the miler type, the 800-meter run puts a great premium on speed, with college-level runners routinely running their first 400 meters in 53 to 55 seconds and world-class runners coming close to averaging 50 seconds per lap.

This emphasis on speed often overshadows the fact that the half-mile distance also requires significant endurance. While this may seem obvious, since the 800 meters is twice as long as the 400, the difference is more than merely quantitative. There are major alterations in training as well, including long stamina runs, paced strength runs, and frequent, slower repetitions of between 100 and 400 meters with moderate recoveries.

Endurance is also needed for another reason, one that is often overlooked. Most major half-mile championships require from one to three preliminary heats before the final; Olympic Games and World Championships require an athlete to run four world-class efforts in five days. Racing strength to meet this challenge has to be trained into the runner or his speed will be no use to him. Strength to run the half-mile cannot be gained in a single season. We firmly believe that consistency is more important than occasional moments of brilliance when training for track racing at distances of 800 meters and above.

One other potential problem affects half-milers more often than sprinters: Specialists at this distance are often "close enough" to distance runners to be called upon to participate in cross-country racing during the season. If the same runners are also expected to compete in the indoor season at the middle distances, they will be racing and training hard during a period when they should be building a foundation. Careful planning for several months in advance and constant vigilance as the schedules are followed allow a half-miler to run the cross-country and indoor seasons without being "flattened" for the important outdoor season. To help deal with these issues, we offer training alternatives in the following schedules for runners who have commitments to cross-country and/or indoor competition before the outdoor season begins.

Distances in the schedules are given in yards. Because the metric equivalents are very close to English (yard) distances, times given in these schedules are valid for both. If you are unsure of the relationship between metric and English track distances, see the Glossary.

*Barrie Almond, insurance executive. (Photograph by David Dowd)*

# The Sub-1:50 880 Yards

*You are ready to train for a sub-1:50 880 if you can run:*

*220 yards in 23.5 seconds*
*440 yards in 50 seconds*

Recognizing that an 880-yard runner might have one, two, or three different seasons in a racing year, we have divided the schedules into three categories which reflect the various racing possibilities that might exist:

A. For the athlete who competes in cross-country, indoor track, and outdoor track
B. For the athlete who competes in cross-country and outdoor track
C. For the athlete who competes in indoor and outdoor track

Unless otherwise specified, "R" means jog recovery; when "R" represents a time, the interval should be spent walking or resting.

## Schedule A

### September

Specialized cross-country training, including:
- 2 track days per week
  - 20 × 110 in :17; 110 R
  - 12 × 220 in :36; 220 R

### October

Specialized cross-country training, including:
- 2 track days per week
  - 16 × 220 in :35; 220 R
  - 10 × 330 in :52; 220 R

### November

Specialized cross-country training, including:
- 2 track days per week
  - 16 × 110 in :16; 110 R
  - 10 × 330 in :50; 220 R

## Schedule B

### September

Specialized cross-country training, including:
- 2 track days per week
  - 20 × 110 in :17; 110 R
  - 12 × 220 in :36; 220 R

### October

Specialized cross-country training, including:
- 2 track days per week
  - 16 × 220 in :35; 220 R
  - 10 × 330 in :52; 220 R

### November

Specialized cross-country training, including:
- 2 track days per week
  - 16 × 110 in :16; 110 R
  - 10 × 330 in :50; 220 R

## Schedule C

### September

5 days of running training per week:
- 2 track days
  - 20 × 110 in :17; 110 R
  - 12 × 220 in :36; 220 R
- 1 controlled strength run (5–10 miles) at 6:15 per mile
- 2 runs of medium distance (5–8 miles) with fartlek interval running (440, 550, 660, 770, 880 yards) at moderate speed

### October

5 days of running training per week:
- 2 track days
  - 10 × 330 in :45; :90 R
  - 16 × 110 in :14; 110 R
- 1 controlled strength run (5–10 miles) at 6:00 per mile
- 2 runs of medium distance (5–8 miles) with fartlek intervals (300, 500, 800, 1,000 yards) at moderate speed

### November

5 days of running training per week:
- 2 track days
  - 12 × 110 in :12.5; 330 R
  - ¾ mile in 3:20; 880 in 2:05; 440 in :58; all 880 R

## December

- 1 controlled strength run (5–8 miles) at 5:30–5:45 per mile
- 1 run of medium distance (5–8 miles) with fartlek intervals (300, 500, 800, 1,000 yards) at moderate speed
- 1 maintenance run of 6 miles

## December

6 days of running training per week:
- 3 track days
  - 10 × 330 in :45; 220 R
  - 3 × 660 in 1:26; 660 R
  - 12 × 110 in :12.5; 110 walk R
- 2 runs of medium distance (5–8 miles) at moderate pace
- 1 controlled strength run (3–5 miles) at 5:15–5:30 per mile

## January

6 days of running training per week:
- 3 track days
  - 4 × 660 in 1:25; 660 R
  - 6 × 330 in :39; 330 R
  - 12 × 110 in :12.5; 110 walk R
- 2 maintenance runs of 6 miles
- Competition or time trial at ¾ mile

## December

1st two weeks: *active rest* (light running — 4–6 miles — every other day)
2nd two weeks (5 days of running training per week):
- 3 track days
  - 2 × 660 in 1:28; 660 R
  - 10 × 330 in :50; 220 R
  - 16 × 110 in :15; 110 R
- 1 controlled strength run of 6 miles in 36:00
- 1 easy maintenance run of 8 miles

## January

5 days of running training per week:
- 2 track days
  - 16 × 220 in :30; 220 R
  - 110 in :15; 220 in :31; 330 in :48; 440 in :65; 330 in :44; 220 in :27; 110 in :13; all 330 R
- 1 easy maintenance run of 8 miles
- 1 controlled strength run of 3 miles in 16:00
- 6 miles easy running

## December

1st two weeks: *active rest* (light running — 4–6 miles — every other day)
2nd two weeks (5 days of running training per week):
- 3 track days
  - 2 × 660 in 1:25; 4:00 R
  - 6 × 330 in :38; 2:00 R
  - 2 × 880 in 2:00; 8:00 R
- 1 controlled strength run of 6 miles in 36:00
- 1 easy maintenance run of 8 miles

## January

6 days of running training per week:
- 3 track days
  - 12 × 110 in :12.5; 220 R
  - 8 × 440 in :60; 440 R
  - 3 × 660 in 1:24; 880 R
- 2 maintenance runs of 6 miles
- Competition or time trial at ¾ mile

## Schedule A

### February

6 days of running training per week:
- 3 track days
  - 6 × 330 in :38; 2:00 R
  - 6 × 440 in :55; 440 walk R
  - 2 × ¾ mile in 3:08; 10:00 R
- 2 maintenance runs of 6 miles
- Competition

### March

1st two weeks (5 days of running training per week):
- 2 track days
  - 3 × 660 in 1:24; 660 R
  - 6 × 330 in :38; 2:00 R
- 3 maintenance runs of 4 miles

2nd two weeks: *active rest* (light running — 4-6 miles — every other day)

## Schedule B

### February

Typical week's training program:

*Day*

1. 10 miles easy running
2. ¾ mile in 3:20; 880 in 2:05; 440 in :58; all 880 R
3. 8 miles easy running
4. Rest day
5. 10 × 330 in :45; 220 R
6. 6 miles easy running with fartlek intervals (440, 660, 880 yards) at moderate pace
7. 6 miles in 35:00

### March

1st week:

*Day*

1. 6 miles easy running
2. 12 × 110 in :12.5; 110 walk R
3. 3 miles in 17:00
4. 6 miles easy running
5. 4 × 660 in 1:24; 4:00 R
6. Rest day
7. 6 × 440 in :56; 440 R

## Schedule C

### February

6 days of running training per week:
- 3 track days
  - 6 × 330 *in* :38; 2:00 R
  - 2 × ¾ mile in 3:05; 10:00 R
  - 8 × 440 in :56; 440 walk R
- 2 maintenance runs of 6 miles
- Competition

### March

1st two weeks (5 days of running training per week):
- 2 track days
  - 3 × 660 in 1:24; 660 R
  - 6 × 330 in :38; 2:00 R
- 3 maintenance runs of 4 miles

2nd two weeks: *active rest* (light running — 4-6 miles — every other day)

2nd week:

*Day*

1 8 miles easy running
2 8 × 330 in :40; 440 R
3 4 miles easy running
4 2 × 1,000 in 2:30; 10:00 R
5 3 miles easy running
6 Rest day
7 Competition *or* 880 time trial
Repeat above schedule for remainder of month

## April

Typical week's training program:

*Day*

1 Maintenance run of 6 miles
2 10 × 110 in :12.0; 220 R
3 ¾ mile in 3:03; 10:00 R; 2 × 660 in 1:27; 5:00 R
4 Paced strength run (3–6 miles) at 5:30 per mile
5 6 × 330 in :38; 2:00 R
6 Rest day
7 Competition

## April

Typical week's training program:

*Day*

1 Maintenance run of 6 miles
2 10 × 110 in :12.5; 220 R
3 ¾ mile in 3:05; 10:00 R; 4 × 220 in :26; 440 R
4 Paced strength run (3–6 miles) at 5:30 per mile
5 6 × 330 in :40; 440 R
6 Rest day
7 Competition

## April

Typical week's training program:

*Day*

1 Maintenance run of 6 miles
2 10 × 110 in :12.5; 220 R
3 ¾ mile in 3:08; 10:00 R; 4 × 220 in :26; 440 R
4 Paced strength run (3–6 miles) at 5:30 per mile
5 6 × 330 in :40; 440 R
6 Rest day
7 Competition

# Schedule A

## May

*Typical week's training program:*

*Day*

1 Maintenance run of 6 miles
2 10 × 110 in :12.5; 220 R
3 1,000 in 2:25; 660 in 1:25; 330 in :38; all 6:00 R
4 Maintenance run of 4 miles
5 4 × 440 in :55; 440 walk R
6 Rest day
7 Competition

## June

*Typical week's training program:*

*Day*

1 Maintenance run of 6 miles
2 6 × 220 in :24.5; 3:00 R
3 4 miles in 24:00
4 ¾ mile in 3:00; 10:00 R; 2 × 330 in :39; 1:00 R
5 4 miles easy running
6 Rest day
7 Competition

# Schedule B

## May

*Typical week's training program:*

*Day*

1 Maintenance run of 6 miles
2 10 × 110 in :12.0; 110 walk R
3 1,000 in 2:25; 660 in 1:25; 330 in :38; all 6:00 R
4 Maintenance run of 4 miles
5 4 × 440 in :55; 440 walk R
6 Rest day
7 Competition

## June

*Typical week's training program:*

*Day*

1 Maintenance run of 6 miles
2 6 × 220 in :24.5; 3:00 R
3 4 miles in 24:00
4 ¾ mile in 3:00; 10:00 R; 2 × 330 in :39; 1:00 R
5 4 miles easy running
6 Rest day
7 Competition

# Schedule C

## May

*Typical week's training program:*

*Day*

1 Maintenance run of 6 miles
2 12 × 110 in :13; 110 walk R
3 100 in 2:25; 660 in 1:25; 330 in :38; all 6:00 R
4 Maintenance run of 4 miles
5 4 × 440 in :55; 440 walk R
6 Rest day
7 Competition

## June

*Typical week's training program:*

*Day*

1 Maintenance run of 6 miles
2 6 × 220 in :24.5; 3:00 R
3 4 miles in 24:00
4 ¾ mile in 3:00; 10:00 R; 2 × 330 in :39; 1:00 R
5 4 miles easy running
6 Rest day
7 Competition

The preceding schedules represent typical weeks during the outdoor season, which usually begins in early March or early April (depending on the particular section of the country). The runner must continually evaluate his progress during this competitive season, particularly if he has actively competed in cross-country and indoor competition. The recommended "active rest" phase should be adhered to — even if the runner is eager to charge into the outdoor track season.

It is equally important that the 880 runner use the fall and winter months to build a solid foundation for the important racing that will follow later in the year. While the specialized work cannot be neglected for this event, a championship performer has to "put the running in his legs" so that he always has speed through strength.

*Robert Gray, investor. (Photograph by Bruce Glikin)*

# The 1:50-to-2:05 880 Yards

*You are ready to train for a 1:50-to-2:05 880 yards if you can run:*

*220 yards in 24 to 27.5 seconds*
*440 yards in 51 to 56 seconds*

In this particular schedule — and all that follow — we indicate a range in quality and quantity for all interval workouts. A 1:50 half-miler and a 2:05 half-miler should train differently. Accordingly, a runner who has a personal best of 1:55 for the 880 yards and who is trying to improve should do the upper (or faster) limits of the suggested workout. A runner who has a personal best of 2:05 for 880 yards should do the lower (or slower) limits of the suggested workout.

For example:

Runner A is a 1:55 880-yard runner
Runner B is a 2:05 880-yard runner

A workout calls for 8–10 × 330 in 45 to 50 seconds with 220 yards recovery

Runner A would run 10 × 330 in :45; 220 R
Runner B would run 8 × 330 in :50; 220 R

Runners who fall somewhere between the upper and lower limits should adjust accordingly. For instance, a 2:00 880-yard runner should modify the schedule and run 10 × 330 in 48 seconds with 220 yards recovery.

Again, at this level of ability, we expect that some runners will be called on to race three competitive seasons in a year: cross-country as well as indoor and outdoor track. The schedule is divided into three sections to reflect the following possible season combinations:

A. For the athlete who competes in cross-country, indoor track, and outdoor track
B. For the athlete who competes in cross-country and outdoor track
C. For the athlete who competes in indoor and outdoor track

Unless otherwise specified, "R" means jog recovery; when "R" represents a time, the interval should be spent walking or resting.

## Schedule A

### September

Specialized cross-country training, including:

- 2 track days per week
  - 20 × 110 in :17–:18; 110 R
  - 12 × 220 in :36–:38; 220 R

### October

Specialized cross-country training, including:

- 2 track days per week
  - 16 × 220 in :35–:37; 220 R
  - 10 × 330 in :52–:54; 220 R

### November

Specialized cross-country training, including:

- 2 track days per week
  - 16 × 110 in :16–:17; 110 R
  - 8–10 × 330 in :50–:52; 220 R

## Schedule B

### September

Specialized cross-country training, including:

- 2 track days per week
  - 20 × 110 in :17–:18; 110 R
  - 12 × 220 in :36–:38; 220 R

### October

Specialized cross-country training, including:

- 2 track days per week
  - 16 × 220 in :35–:37; 220 R
  - 10 × 330 in :52–:54; 220 R

### November

Specialized cross-country training, including:

- 2 track days per week
  - 16 × 110 in :16–:17; 110 R
  - 8–10 × 330 in :50–:52; 220 R

## Schedule C

### September

5 days of running training per week:

- 2 track days
  - 20 × 110 in :17–:18; 110 R
  - 12 × 220 in :36–:38; 220 R
  - 1 controlled strength run (5–10 miles) at 6:00–6:30 per mile
  - 2 runs of medium distance (5–7 miles) with fartlek interval running (440, 550, 660, 770, 880 yards) at moderate speed

### October

5 days of running training per week:

- 2 track days
  - 8–10 × 330 in :45–:50; 330 R
  - 16 × 110 in :14–16; 110 R
  - 1 controlled strength run (5–10 miles) at 6:00–6:30 per mile
  - 2 runs of medium distance (5–7 miles) with fartlek intervals (300, 500, 800, 1,000 yards) at moderate speed

### November

5 days of running training per week:

- 2 track days
  - 12 × 110 in :12.5–:13.5; 330 R
  - ¾ mile in 3:20–3:30; 880 in 2:05–2:15; 440 in :59–:66; all 880 R

• 1 strength run (5–8 miles) at 5:35–6:15 per mile
• 2 runs of medium distance (5–7 miles) with fartlek intervals (300, 500, 800, 1,000 yards) at moderate speed

## December

6 days of running training per week:
• 3 track days
  • 8–10 × 330 in :45–:50; 220 R
  • 3 × 660 in 1:27–1:37; 660 R
  • 12 × 110 in :12.5–:14; 110 walk R
• 2 runs of medium distance (5–7 miles) at moderate pace
• 1 paced run (3–5 miles) at 5:20–6:00 per mile

## January

6 days of running training per week:
• 2 maintenance runs of 6 miles
• 3 track days
  • 12 × 110 in :12.5–:13.5; 110 walk R
  • 6 × 330 in :39–:43; 2:00 R
  • 4 × 660 in 1:26–1:35; 3:00 R
• Competition or time trial at ¾ mile

## December

1st 2 weeks: *active rest* (light running — 4–6 miles — every other day)
2nd two weeks (5 days of running training per week):
• 2 track days
  • 16 × 110 in :16–:17; 110 R
  • 8–10 × 330 in :50–:52; 220 R
• 2 maintenance runs of 7 miles
• 1 paced run of 6 miles in 36:00–37:30

## January

Typical week's training program:

Day
1 8 miles easy running
2 12–16 × 220 in :30–:32; 220 R
3 110 in :15–:17; 220 in :31–:33; 330 in :48–:51; 440 in :65–:68; 330 in :44–:46; 220 in :28–:31; 110 in :13–:14; all 330 R
4 Rest day
5 3 miles in 16:30–17:30
6 6 miles easy running
7 Rest day

## December

1st two weeks: *active rest* (light running — 4–6 miles — every other day)
2nd two weeks (5 days of running training per week):
• 3 track days
  • 2 × 660 in 1:26–1:36; 4:00 R
  • 4–6 × 330 in :39–:44; 440 R
  • 2 × 880 in 2:02–2:16; 8:00 R
• 1 paced run of 6 miles in 36:00–37:30
• 1 maintenance run of 8 miles

## January

6 days of running training per week:
• 2 maintenance runs of 6 miles
• 3 track days
  • 12 × 110 in :12.5–:13.5; 220 R
  • 8 × 440 in :60–:65; 440 R
  • 3 × 660 in 1:26–1:35; 880 R
• Competition or time trial at ¾ mile

## Schedule A

*February*

Typical week's training program:

*Day*

1 6 miles easy running
2 6 × 330 in :39–:43; 2:00 R
3 2 × ¾ mile in 3:10–3:30; 10:00 R
4 6 miles easy running
5 6 × 440 in :55–:60; 440 R
6 Rest day
7 Competition

*March*

1st two weeks (5 days of running training per week):
• 2 maintenance runs of 6 miles
• 2 track days
  • 3 × 660 in 1:25–1:34; 660 R
  • 6 × 330 in :38.5–:42; 2:00 R
• 2 rest days
• Competition
2nd two weeks: *active rest* (6 miles easy running every other day)

## Schedule B

*February*

Typical week's training program:

*Day*

1 10 miles easy running
2 ¾ mile in 3:20–3:35; 880 in 2:06–2:14; 440 in :58–:63; all 880 R
3 8 miles easy running
4 Rest day
5 8–10 × 330 in :45–:48; 220 R
6 6 miles easy running with fartlek intervals (440, 660, 880 yards)
7 6 miles in 35:00–36:30

*March*

1st week:

*Day*

1 6 miles easy running
2 12 × 110 in :13–:14; 110 walk R
3 3 miles in 17:00–18:00
4 6 miles easy running
5 4 × 660 in 1:25–1:34; 4:00 R
6 Rest day
7 Competition

## Schedule C

*February*

Typical week's training program:

*Day*

1 6 miles easy running
2 6 × 330 in :39–:43; 2:00 R
3 2 × ¾ mile in 3:10–3:30; 10:00 R
4 6 miles easy running
5 6–8 × 440 in :57–:62; 440 walk R
6 Rest day
7 Competition

*March*

1st two weeks (5 days of running training per week):
• 2 maintenance runs of 6 miles
• 2 track days
  • 3 × 660 in 1:25–1:34; 660 R
  • 6 × 330 in :38.5–:42; 2:00 R
• 2 rest days
• Competition
2nd two weeks: *active rest* (6 miles easy running every other day)

2nd week:

*Day*

1 8 miles easy running
2 8 × 330 in :40–:44; 440 R
3 4 miles easy running
4 2 × 1,000 in 2:32–2:45; 10:00 R
5 3 miles easy running
6 Rest day
7 Competition *or* 880 time trial
Repeat above schedule for remainder of month

*April*

Typical week's training program:

*Day*

1 Maintenance run of 6 miles
2 10 × 110 in :12.5–:13.5; 220 R
3 ¾ mile in 3:10–3:20; 10:00 R; 4 × 220 in :26–:28; 440 R
4 Paced strength run (3–6 miles) at 5:30–6:00 per mile
5 6 × 330 in :40–:43; 440 R
6 Rest day
7 Competition

*April*

Typical week's training program:

*Day*

1 Maintenance run of 6 miles
2 10 × 110 in :12.5–:13.5; 220 R
3 ¾ mile in 3:05–3:15; 10:00 R; 2 × 660 in 1:28–1:34; 5:00 R
4 Paced strength run (3–6 miles) at 5:30–6:00 per mile
5 6 × 330 in :39–:42; 2:00 R
6 Rest day
7 Competition

*April*

Typical week's training program:

*Day*

1 Maintenance run of 6 miles
2 10 × 110 in :12.5–:13.5; 220 R
3 ¾ mile in 3:05–3:15; 10:00 R; 4 × 220 in :27–:29; 440 R
4 Paced strength run (3–6 miles) at 5:30–6:00 per mile
5 6 × 330 in :40–:43; 440 R
6 Rest day
7 Competition

## Schedule A

*May*

Typical week's training program:

*Day*

1 Maintenance run of 6 miles
2 4 × 440 in :55–:59; 440 walk R
3 1,000 in 2:28–2:42; 660 in 1:26–1:34; 330 in :39–:42; all 6:00 R
4 Paced strength run of 3 miles at 5:45–6:00 per mile
5 12 × 110 in :13–:14.5; 220 R
6 Rest day
7 Competition

*June*

Typical week's training program:

*Day*

1 6 miles easy running
2 6 × 220 in :25–:28; 3:00 R
3 ¾ mile in 3:02–3:12; 10:00 R; 2 × 330 in :40–:43; 440 R
4 6 miles easy running
5 3 miles at 5:30–6:00 per mile
6 Rest day
7 Competition

## Schedule B

*May*

Typical week's training program:

*Day*

1 Maintenance run of 6 miles
2 4 × 440 in :55–:59; 440 walk R
3 1,000 in 2:28–2:42; 660 in 1:26–1:34; 330 in :39–:42; all 6:00 R
4 Paced strength run of 3 miles at 5:45–6:00 per mile
5 12 × 110 in :13–:14.5; 220 R
6 Rest day
7 Competition

*June*

Typical week's training program:

*Day*

1 6 miles easy running
2 6 × 220 in :25–:28; 3:00 R
3 ¾ mile in 3:02–3:12; 10:00 R; 2 × 330 in :40–:43; 440 R
4 6 miles easy running
5 3 miles at 5:30–6:00 per mile
6 Rest day
7 Competition

## Schedule C

*May*

Typical week's training program:

*Day*

1 Maintenance run of 6 miles
2 4 × 440 in :55–:59; 440 walk R
3 1,000 in 2:28–2:42; 660 in 1:26–1:34; 330 in :39–:42; all 6:00 R
4 Paced strength run of 3 miles at 5:45–6:00 per mile
5 12 × 110 in :13–:14.5; 220 R
6 Rest day
7 Competition

*June*

Typical week's training program:

*Day*

1 6 miles easy running
2 6 × 220 in :25–:28; 3:00 R
3 ¾ mile in 3:02–3:12; 10:00 R; 2 × 330 in :40–:43; 440 R
4 6 miles easy running
5 3 miles at 5:30–6:00 per mile
6 Rest day
7 Competition

An 880-yard specialist needs to continually evaluate himself throughout the outdoor track season — particularly if he has raced a cross-country and/or an indoor track season. The "active rest" periods after each season must be adhered to if the athlete expects to be in peak form during the championship weeks.

*Mark Scheid, university professor. (Photograph by Photo Systems, Inc.)*

# The 2:06-to-2:20 880 Yards

*You are ready to train for a 2:06-to-2:20 880 yards if you can run:*

*220 yards in 27.5 to 30 seconds*
*440 yards in 57 to 62.5 seconds*

Once again the competitive categories are divided into:

A. For the athlete who competes in cross-country, indoor track, and outdoor track
B. For the athlete who competes in cross-country and outdoor track
C. For the athlete who competes in indoor and outdoor track

Unless otherwise specified, "R" means jog recovery; when "R" represents a time, the interval should be spent walking or jogging.

## Schedule A

*September*

Specialized cross-country training, including:

- 2 track days per week
  - 20 × 110 in :17.5–:18.5; 110 R
  - 12 × 220 in :37–:39; 220 R

*October*

Specialized cross-country training, including:

- 2 track days per week
  - 16 × 220 in :36–:38; 220 R
  - 8–10 × 330 in :53–:55; 220 R

## Schedule B

*September*

Specialized cross-country training, including:

- 2 track days per week
  - 20 × 110 in :17.5–:18.5; 110 R
  - 12 × 220 in :37–:39; 220 R

*October*

Specialized cross-country training, including:

- 2 track days per week
  - 16 × 220 in :36–:38; 220 R
  - 8–10 × 330 in :53–:55; 220 R

## Schedule C

*September*

5 days of running training per week:

- 2 track days
  - 20 × 110 in :17.5–:18.5; 110 R
  - 12 × 220 in :37–:39; 220 R
  - 1 controlled strength run (5–7 miles) at 6:00–6:30 per mile
  - 2 runs of medium distance (5–7 miles) with fartlek intervals (440, 550, 660, 770, 880 yards) at moderate speed

*October*

5 days of running training per week:

- 2 track days
  - 16 × 110 in :16–:17; 110 R
  - 8–10 × 330 in :50–:54; 330 R
  - 1 controlled strength run (5–10 miles) at 6:00–6:45 per mile
  - 2 runs of medium distance (5–7 miles) with fartlek intervals (300, 500, 800, 1,000 yards) at moderate speed

November

Specialized cross-country training, including:

• 2 track days per week
  • 16 × 110 in :17–:18; 110 R
  • 8–10 × 330 in :51–:53; 220 R

December

1st two weeks: *active rest* (light running — 4–6 miles — every other day)
2nd two weeks (5 days of running training per week):

• 3 track days
  • 2 × 660 in 1:37–1:47; 660 R
  • 4–6 × 330 in :45–:50; 440 R
  • 2 × 880 in 2:18–2:30; 880 R
• 1 6-mile strength run in 37:30–39:00
• 6 miles easy running

November

Specialized cross-country training, including:

• 2 track days per week
  • 16 × 110 in :17–:18; 110 R
  • 8–10 × 330 in :51–:53; 220 R

December

1st two weeks: *active rest* (light running — 4–6 miles — every other day)
2nd two weeks (5 days of running training per week):

• 2 track days
  • 16 × 110 in :17–:18; 110 R
  • 8–10 × 330 in :53–:56; 220 R
• 2 maintenance runs of 7 miles at easy pace
• 1 6-mile strength run in 37:30–39:00

November

5 days of running training per week:

• 2 tracks days
  • 12 × 110 in :13–:14.5; 330 R
  • ¾ mile in 3:33–3:45; 880 in 2:18–2:30; 440 in :66–:73; all 880 R
• 1 controlled strength run (5–8 miles) at 6:00–6:30 per mile
• 2 runs of medium distance (5–7 miles) with fartlek intervals (300, 500, 800, 1,000 yards) at moderate speed

December

6 days of running training per week:

• 3 track days
  • 8–10 x 330 in :51–:53; 220 R
  • 3 × 660 in 1:37–1:47; 660 R
  • 12 × 110 in :13–:14.5; 110 walk R
• 2 runs of medium distance (5–7 miles) at moderate speed
• 1 controlled strength run (3–5 miles) at 5:45–6:15 per mile

## Schedule A

*January*

Typical week's training program:

*Day*

1. 6 miles easy running
2. 6 × 330 in :44–:49; 440 R
3. 2 × ¾ mile in 3:30–3:45; 10:00 R
4. 6 miles easy running
5. 6 × 440 in :61–:67; 660 R
6. Rest day
7. Competition

*February*

Typical week's training program:

*Day*

1. 6 miles easy running
2. 6 × 330 in :44–:49; 440 R
3. 8–12 × 110 in :13.5–:14.5; 220 R
4. 6 miles easy running
5. 4–6 × 440 in :61–:67; 660 R
6. Rest day
7. Competition

## Schedule B

*January*

Typical week's training program:

*Day*

1. 10 miles easy running
2. ¾ mile in 3:35–3:45; 880 in 2:15–2:28; 440 in :64–:69; all 880 R
3. 8 miles easy running
4. Rest day
5. 8–10 × 330 in :49–:52; 220 R
6. Medium-distance (5 miles) run with fartlek intervals (440, 660, 880 yards) at moderate speed
7. 6 miles in 36:30–37:30

*February*

Typical week's training program:

*Day*

1. 10 miles easy running
2. ¾ mile in 3:35–3:45; 5:00 R; 8–10 × 220 in :33–:35; 220 walk R
3. 6 miles easy running
4. 8–12 × 110 in :13.5–:14.5; 220 R
5. 6 miles easy running
6. Rest day
7. 3 miles in 17:00–17:30

## Schedule C

*January*

Typical week's training program:

*Day*

1. 6 miles easy running
2. 6 × 330 in :44–:49; 440 R
3. 6 miles easy running
4. 6–8 × 440 in :63–:68; 440 walk R
5. 6 miles easy running
6. Rest day
7. Competition

*February*

Typical week's training program:

*Day*

1. 6 miles easy running
2. 8–12 × 110 in :13.5–:14.5; 220 R
3. 2 × ¾ mile in 3:30–3:45; 10:00 R
4. 4 miles easy running
5. 6–8 × 440 in :63–:69; 440 walk R
6. Rest day
7. Competition

## March

1st two weeks (4 days of running training per week):

- 2 maintenance runs of 6 miles at easy pace
- 2 track days
  - 3 × 660 in 1:35–1:47; 660 R
  - 6 × 330 in :40–:44; 2:00 R
- 2 rest days
- Competition

2nd two weeks: *active rest* (6 miles easy running every other day)

## April

Typical week's training program:

Day
1 6 miles easy running
2 10 × 110 in :13.5–:15.0; 220 R
3 ¾ mile in 3:23–3:45; 10:00 R; 4 × 220 in :29–:32; 440 R
4 Strength run of 3–6 miles at 5:50–6:20 per mile
5 6 × 330 in :44–:49; 440 R
6 Rest day
7 Competition

## March

1st week:

Day
1 6 miles easy running
2 12 × 110 in :14–:15; 110 walk R
3 3 miles in 18:00–18:30
4 6 miles easy running
5 4 × 660 in 1:35–1:47; 4:00 R
6 Rest day
7 Competition

2nd week:

Day
1 8 miles easy running
2 8 × 330 in :45–:49; 440 R
3 4 miles easy running
4 2 × 1,000 in 2:45–3:06; 10:00 R
5 3 miles easy running
6 Rest day
7 Competition *or* 880 time trial

## April

Typical week's training program:

Day
1 6 miles easy running
2 12 × 110 in :14–:15; 220 R
3 ¾ mile in 3:17–3:42; 10:00 R; 2 × 660 in 1:35–1:43; 5:00 R
4 Strength run of 3–6 miles at 5:50–6:20 per mile
5 6 × 330 in :43–:48; 2:00 R
6 Rest day
7 Competition

## March

1st two weeks (5 days of running training per week):

- 2 maintenance runs of 6 miles at easy pace
- 2 track days
  - 3 × 660 in 1:35–1:47; 660 R
  - 6 × 330 in :40–:44; 2:00 R
- 2 rest days
- Competition

2nd two weeks: *active rest* (6 miles easy running every other day)

## April

Typical week's training program:

Day
1 6 miles easy running
2 10 × 110 in :13.5–:15; 220 R
3 ¾ mile in 3:17–3:42; 10:00 R; 4 × 220 in :29–:32; 440 R
4 Strength run of 3–6 miles at 5:50–6:20 per mile
5 6 × 330 in :44–:49; 440 R
6 Rest day
7 Competition

## Schedule A

*May*

Typical week's training program:

*Day*

1 6 miles easy running
2 4 × 440 in :60–:66; 440 walk R
3 1,000 in 2:45–3:05; 660 in 1:35–1:45; 330 in :43–:47; all 6:00 R
4 3-mile strength run at 5:50–6:15 per mile
5 12 × 110 in :15–16.5; 220 R
6 Rest day
7 Competition

*June*

Typical week's training program:

*Day*

1 6 miles easy running
2 6 × 220 in :28–:31; 3:00 R
3 ¾ mile in 3:15–3:37; 10:00 R; 2 × 330 in :44–:48; 440 R
4 5 miles easy running
5 3 miles at 5:45–6:00 per mile
6 Rest day
7 Competition

## Schedule B

*May*

Typical week's training program:

*Day*

1 6 miles easy running
2 4 × 440 in :60–:66; 440 walk R
3 1,000 in 2:45–3:05; 660 in 1:35–1:45; 330 in :43–:47; all 6:00 R
4 3-mile strength run at 5:50–6:15 per mile
5 12 × 110 in :15–16.5; 220 R
6 Rest day
7 Competition

*June*

Typical week's training program:

*Day*

1 6 miles easy running
2 6 × 220 in :28–:31; 3:00 R
3 ¾ mile in 3:15–3:37; 10:00 R; 2 × 330 in :44–:48; 440 R
4 5 miles easy running
5 3 miles at 5:45–6:00 per mile
6 Rest day
7 Competition

## Schedule C

*May*

Typical week's training program:

*Day*

1 6 miles easy running
2 4 × 440 in :60–:66; 440 walk R
3 1,000 in 2:45–3:05; 660 in 1:35–1:45; 330 in :43–:47; all 6:00 R
4 3-mile strength run at 5:50–6:15 per mile
5 12 × 110 in :15–16.5; 220 R
6 Rest day
7 Competition

*June*

Typical week's training program:

*Day*

1 6 miles easy running
2 6 × 220 in :28–:31; 3:00 R
3 ¾ mile in 3:15–3:37; 10:00 R; 2 × 330 in :44–:48; 440 R
4 5 miles easy running
5 3 miles at 5:45–6:00 per mile
6 Rest day
7 Competition

*Georgette Green, special education teacher. (Photograph by Bruce Glikin)*

# The 2:21-to-2:40 880 Yards

*You are ready to train for a 2:21-to-2:40 880 yards if you can run:*

*220 yards in 30.5 to 33 seconds*
*440 yards in 63 to 70 seconds*

For the runner who feels a need for a change in her running life and who believes that she has discovered (or possesses) a measure of speed in her training or racing, the time might be right to pit herself against the half-mile distance. In general, the time range above for this schedule is not quite of the standard that should convince an individual to specialize at this distance (except for a small group, e.g., high school girls and some masters men and women), but it is an appropriate standard to justify experimentation with shorter-distance racing.

While we would expect the majority of runners to find the main benefits of training for the 880 at this time standard to be change and variety, there will be a substantial number of runners who will achieve (and exceed) the lower (2:21) range. Runners in this group might then consider specializing at the 880 distance and begin the appropriate schedule the following September. You might wish to try the 880-yard distance for a variety of reasons:

- you have achieved the "ready to train" time standards at 220 and 440 yards
- you want to race at a variety of distances in your competitive program
- you find that in most of your races you have the ability to muster fast finishing "kicks"
- you find you have excellent early speed in your races but peter out as the race progresses
- you want to improve your overall speed through short-distance racing in order to improve at the longer distances
- you were considered more a sprinter during junior and senior high school
- you find it easier to train for and race shorter distances during hot-weather months
- you appreciate challenge and change in your running life

Once you have made the decision to begin training for the 880 distance, be aware that the conversion from longer-distance training and racing will not be without some inconvenience. We will presume that you are somewhat deficient on short and medium endurance (aerobic conditioning) and significantly deficient in anaerobic conditioning.

The first six weeks of conditioning prior to the beginning of the racing season and the final six weeks of specialized training concentrate on easing the runner through the physiological adaptation to the shorter distances. The initial conditioning, however, still has a variety of the components (stamina, strength runs, maintenance runs, aerobic and anaerobic intervals, and fartlek running) that compose all schedules for this distance.

"Easy running" in this schedule is 7:15 to 8:15 per mile. "R" stands for jog recovery unless otherwise specified; when "R" represents a time, the interval should be spent walking or resting.

The following is a typical 14-day training program during the six-week conditioning phase:

*Day*

1 8 miles easy running
2 12 × 110 in :16–:17.5; 330 R
3 3–5 miles at 6:00–6:30 per mile
4 5 miles easy running
5 6 × 330 in :50–:55; 440 R
6 Rest day
7 3 × 660 in 1:52–2:06; 880 R
8 7 miles easy running
9 12–16 × 220 in :36–:39; 220 R
10 4 miles easy running
11 3–5 miles at 6:00–6:15 per mile
12 ¾ mile in 3:52–4:15; 880 in 2:30–2:48; 440 in :70–:75; all 880 R
13 4 miles easy running
14 6 miles easy running with fartlek intervals (200, 300, and 400 yards)

After the first fourteen days, the following track workouts may be substituted on any of the track days (do only *one* of the following per workout):

• 6–8 × 440 in :69–:75; 440 walk R
• 2 × ¾ mile in 3:45–4:15; 10:00 R
• 6 × 220 in :32–:35; 440 walk R
• 10 × 110 in :16–:17; 110 R

The next six weeks comprise specialized training for, and the beginning of racing at, the 880-yard distance.

## 1st Week

*Day*
1  8 miles easy running
2  8 × 330 in :50–:54; 220 walk R
3  3 miles at 5:50–6:10 per mile
4  4 miles easy running
5  2 × 660 in 1:48–2:03; 660 R
6  Rest day
7  880 race *or* 1,000-yard time trial

## 2nd Week

*Day*
1  6 miles easy running
2  6 × 220 in :33.5–:35.5; 440 walk R
3  4 miles easy running
4  2 × 1,000 in 3:10–3:30; 880 R
5  10 × 110 in :16–:17; 220 R
6  Rest day
7  Race *or* 880 time trial

## 3rd Week

*Day*
1  6 miles easy running
2  ¾ mile in 3:45–4:05; 10:00 R;
   2 × 660 in 1:48–2:03; 10:00 R
3  3 miles easy running
4  10 × 220 in :35–:38; 440 R
5  4 miles at 6:30–7:00 per mile
6  3 miles easy running
7  Race

## 4th Week

*Day*
1  6 miles easy running
2  6 × 330 in :51–:55; 440 R
3  3–5 miles at 6:00–6:15 per mile
4  6 × 440 in :70–:76; 440 walk R
5  Rest day
6  3 miles easy running
7  Race *or* ¾-mile time trial

## 5th Week

*Day*
1  6 miles easy running
2  8 × 110 in :15.5–:16.5; 110 walk R
3  4 miles at 6:10–6:20 per mile
4  2 × 660 in 1:48–2:03; 440 walk R
5  5 miles easy running
6  Rest day
7  Competition

## 6th Week

*Day*
1  6 miles easy running
2  8 × 220 in :34–:37; 220 walk R
3  5 miles easy running
4  6 × 440 in :70–:76; 440 walk R
5  Rest day
6  2–3 miles easy running
7  Competition

After six weeks of specialized training and racing, the runner is in a position to evaluate her progress and ascertain whether the 880 yards is indeed the event she is best suited for. Should this be the case, go to the appropriate year-round 880-yard schedule.

*Melissa Lyon-Simon, investment executive. (Photograph by Bruce Glikin)*

# The 2:41-to-3:00 880 Yards

*You are ready to train for a 2:41-to-3:00 880 yards if you can run:*

*220 yards in 34.5 to 39 seconds*
*440 yards in 72 to 81 seconds*

This schedule is the break-off point for specific 880-yard training for competition by the self-coached runner. Although slower runners might try training for the 880 yards to add some variety to their running programs, the reality is that a runner who cannot achieve the above standards just does not have the necessary speed to be successful in this event. This does not mean that individuals in this category cannot be eminently successful at longer distances.

We again recommend an initial six-week conditioning period with a variety of training components (strength runs, stamina runs, aerobic and anaerobic intervals, and fartlek intervals) before beginning a specialized 880-yard training program.

As suggested in earlier schedules, runners converting their training to this shorter distance should adjust the training times and number of repetitions undertaken to complement their particular position on the time spread for the suggested standards. Therefore, a runner who has clocked a 34.5-second 220 yards and 72 seconds for 440 yards would do the upper (or faster) limits of the workout 12–16 × 220 yards in 37.5 to 41.5 seconds with 220 yards recovery. Thus his workout would be 16 × 220 in 37.5 seconds with 220 yards recovery. A runner who just achieves the lower (or slower) limits of the time spread should interpret this workout to be 12 × 220 yards in 41.5 seconds with 220 yards recovery. A runner who falls somewhere between the upper and lower limits should adjust the times and number of repetitions accordingly. "Easy running" in this schedule is 7:30 to 8:30 per mile. "R" means jog recovery unless otherwise specified; when "R" represents a time, the interval should be spent walking or resting. A typical fourteen-day training program during this phase of conditioning is shown on the next page.

*Day*

1  8 miles easy running
2  12 × 110 in :18–:19.5; 330 R
3  3–5 miles at 6:30–7:00 per mile
4  5 miles easy running
5  6 × 330 in :56–:62; 440 R
6  Rest day
7  3 × 660 in 2:05–2:20; 880 R
8  6 miles easy running
9  12–16 × 220 in :39–:43.5; 220 R

10  3 miles easy running
11  3–5 miles at 6:30–6:45 per mile
12  ¾ mile in 4:18–4:45; 880 in 2:50–3:10; 440 in :76–:85; all 880 R
13  4 miles easy running
14  6 miles easy running with fartlek intervals (200, 300, and 400 yards)

After the initial fourteen days, the following track workouts may be substituted on any of the track days of the remaining four-week conditioning period (do only *one* of the following per track workout):

• 6–8 × 440 in :76–:85; 440 walk R
• 2 × ¾ mile in 4:15–4:42; 10:00 R
• 6 × 220 in :35.5–:40; 440 walk R
• 10 × 110 in :17.5–:19.5; 110 R

The next six weeks comprise specialized training and the beginning of racing at the 880-yard/800-meter distance.

## 1st Week

*Day*

1  7 miles easy running
2  8 × 330 in :55–:65; 220 walk R
3  3 miles at 6:15–6:45 per mile
4  4 miles easy running
5  2 × 660 in 2:02–2:18; 660 R
6  Rest day
7  880 competition *or* 1,000-yard time trial

## 2nd Week

*Day*

1  6 miles easy running
2  6 × 220 in :35.5–:39.5; 440 walk R
3  4 miles easy running
4  2 × 1,000 in 3:30–4:00; 880 R
5  10 × 110 in :17.5–:19.5; 220 R

6  Rest day
7  Competition *or* 880 time trial

## 3rd Week

*Day*

1  6 miles easy running
2  ¾ mile in 4:05–4:15; 10:00 R; 2 × 660 in 2:04–2:18; 10:00 R
3  3 miles easy running
4  10 × 220 in :35.5–:39.5; 440 R
5  4 miles at 7:00–7:30 per mile
6  3 miles easy running
7  Competition

## 4th Week

*Day*

1  6 miles easy running
2  6 × 330 in :55–:64; 440 R
3  3–5 miles at 6:15–6:45 per mile

4  6 × 440 in :76–:85; 440 walk R
5  Rest day
6  3 miles easy running
7  Competition *or* ¾-mile time trial

## 5th Week

*Day*

1  6 miles easy running
2  8 × 110 in :17–:19; 110 walk R
3  4 miles at 6:15–6:30 per mile
4  2 × 660 in 2:03–2:18; 440 walk R
5  4 miles easy running

6  Rest day
7  Competition

## 6th Week

*Day*

1  6 miles easy running
2  8 × 220 in :37–:42; 220 walk R
3  4 miles easy running
4  6 × 440 in :76–:85; 440 walk R
5  Rest day
6  2–3 miles easy running
7  Competition

*Roger Bannister breaks the tape in history's first sub-4-minute mile.*
(*Photograph courtesy of* Track and Field News)

# FIVE

# 1,500 Meters — 1 Mile

IN THE FIRST CHAPTER, WE DISCUSSED the fact that most of the participants in American road races are running the wrong distances and are physiologically better equipped to race shorter distances. Many self-coached runners intuitively sense this, but at the same time they are not at all sure that they have the speed to be competitive at shorter distances. You may have experienced — in races, on the racquetball or tennis court, or in other sports — that depressing moment of truth when someone "leaves you for dead" in the space of 10 or 20 yards. You know then that you do not have the inherent speed of the true sprinter. You may have also concluded that you had better stick to long races — the longer the better.

Fortunately, that conclusion is not necessarily warranted. "Pure" speed of the type that marks the great sprinters is usually a liability at distances longer than a quarter-mile, simply because the muscle fibers that produce it fatigue so quickly and are slow to recharge. (Many of the best sprinters we know consider the quarter-mile the most grueling event in sports. For them, of course, it is.) A Carl Lewis or a Kirk Baptiste could never be a world-class miler, in spite of — and because of — his natural speed.

The average American road racer may not make the distinction between the sprints and the mile simply because to him or her they are all intervals that are run in training. But to the track-trained athlete, the difference is pronounced. As we mentioned in the previous chapter, even the body types of the sprinter and the miler differ, the sprinter being powerfully built and explosive, the miler typically smaller and lighter but taller for his weight. The half-mile and the mile are usually distinguished from the sprints by being called middle-distance races; they were named in an era when "distance" races began at 2 miles.

So you don't need pure speed to be a good miler. But you *do* need to train to run fast, and your ability to do that can be improved by careful attention to biomechanics, relaxation, and acceleration in the fast workouts you will have to run to race a mile.

As we noted in our first book, it is a common error to assume that a runner who lacks natural speed will need to do more speed training (to make up for his natural deficiency) than a runner who is naturally gifted. In practice, however, your ability to tolerate the intensity of speed workouts is limited by your FT/ST ratio: A naturally fast runner can tolerate more speed work than a naturally slower runner. If the slower runner attempts too much speed work, he will break down under the stress.

To determine how much speed work is feasible in your training, consult the following chart:

|  |  | *Males* | *Females* |
|---|---|---|---|
| Alpha | 100 meters | 11.5–13.0 seconds | 12.5–14.0 seconds |
|  | 200 meters | 23.4–26.9 seconds | 26.0–29.0 seconds |
| Beta | 100 meters | 13.1–14.5 seconds | 14.1–15.5 seconds |
|  | 200 meters | 27.0–30.0 seconds | 29.1–32.0 seconds |
| Gamma | 100 meters | 14.6–16.0 seconds | 15.6–17.0 seconds |
|  | 200 meters | 30.1–33.0 seconds | 32.1–35.0 seconds |

If you can qualify as an alpha-level athlete, you should be able to tolerate four to five quality speed sessions during a two-week period. This does *not* mean that you will always run that many or that you *must* run that many. Five speed sessions per fourteen-day period are recommended for mile and 1,500-meter training. Four speed sessions should be used over the same period in training for events from 3,000 meters to 8,000 meters (5 miles). Alphas should run three speed sessions in two weeks when training for distances from 10,000 meters to the marathon (the specific type of speed training will also be affected by the distance of the event you are training for).

A beta-level runner can tolerate three or four speed sessions every fourteen days. Typically he or she will schedule four when training for the 1,500-meter/1-mile race, three when training for 3,000 to 8,000 meters, and two when planning to race at distances from 10,000 meters to the marathon.

Gamma runners can run two to three quality speed sessions every fourteen days. They will usually plan on running three when training for the 1,500 meter/1 mile, two when training for 3,000 to 8,000 meters, and one and a half (three a month) when training to race between 10,000 meters and the marathon.

## Converting Metric to Mile Times

To Americans, the mile is the king of track events. We remember the names of the great milers, both American and non-American: Nurmi, Anderson, Haaeg, Bannister, Landy, Elliott, Snell, Ryun, Liquori, Hilton, Walker, Coe, Ovett, Cram. Our use of the mile as the standard is even more evident in the case of Glenn Cunningham, who held the world record at 800 meters, not the mile, but is more often remembered as the greatest American miler of his day. We even call the 1,500 meters the metric mile, since it is only 119.6 yards short of a mile.

The mile is also the standard distance by which we measure runs. This is perhaps clearest in the road-racing events. Nearly all are metric — 8K, 10K, 15K, and so on — but every runner judges his or her pace by calculating *mile* splits.

Because of the great miling tradition, the mile run is the only non-metric event still raced in international track (omitting the marathon, which, properly speaking, is neither a metric distance nor an English one). Thus the mile is sometimes run even in countries that have never used the English system of measurement. The most notable example is Norway, where Bislett Stadium in Oslo has seen almost all of the recent world mile records, including Steve Cram's 3:46. On the other hand, the mile is *not* raced at the NCAA and The Athletics Congress championships, nor at many major regional and conference championships, where it is replaced by the "international" distance of 1,500 meters.

Because of this duality, the need for a standard to compare mile times to 1,500-meter times is obvious. It is a common rule of thumb to add 17 seconds to a 1,500-meter time to get the comparable mile time. While this method is reasonably accurate for mile times around

*Two great milers with great natural speed: Steve Cram (325), current world-record holder in the mile and member of the world-record 4 × 800-meter relay team, and Steve Ovett (341), former mile world-record holder and gold medalist at 800 meters in Moscow. (Photograph by George Herringshaw; courtesy* Track and Field News)

4 minutes, it is increasingly inaccurate for slower runners, since it is unlikely that a 5-minute miler would run the 119.6 yards as fast as a 4-minute miler can.

*Track and Field News,* for years the bible of the sport, and the prime source for all track statistics, suggests that a better estimate can be achieved by multiplying the 1,500-meter time by 1.08. Thus a 1,500-meter time of 3:29.67 (Cram's former world record) is equal to a 3:46.4 for a mile — very close to the actual time Cram ran in his record mile (3:46.31). But Tatyana Kazankina's 1,500-meter world record (3:52.47) works out to a mile of 4:11, rather than the 4:09 she is usually credited with by the 17-second rule. To convert a mile time to a 1,500-meter time, multiply the mile time in seconds by 0.926 (the reciprocal of 1.08). Using this standard, the all-important 4-minute mile is equivalent to a 3:42.24 1,500-meter race:

4 minutes = 240 seconds

$240 \times 0.926 = 222.24$ seconds = 3:42.24

*Leonard Hilton, early in his career, sitting on Villanova's Marty Liquori. (Photograph courtesy Leonard Hilton)*

# The 4:00 Mile or 3:42 1,500 Meters

*You are ready to train for a 4:00 mile if you can run:*

*220 yards in 23.8 seconds*
*440 yards in 52 seconds*

*To run a 4:00 mile, you will need to average 60 seconds per quarter*

When English professional runner Walter George set a mile record of 4:12¾ * in 1886 during a match race against Scotsman William Cummings, speculation began as to whether man could ever run a mile in 4 minutes. Despite the interest in this topic, George's record was not bettered for twenty-nine years, and by 1943 the record for the mile had been reduced by only 11.2 seconds. Not until 1953, almost seventy years after George's historic effort, was it clear that the 4-minute mile was a definite possibility.

The mythic aura of the 4-minute mile was in part a result of this nearly three-quarters of a century of speculation. Because man had run so close to it, and yet it remained out of reach so long, physiologists speculated that the 15-mile-an-hour pace necessary was the very limit of human endurance. Therefore, given the variabilities of track, weather, and human frailty, the sub-4-minute mile was probably "impossible."

In 1953, a trio of milers around the world (Wes Santee, United States; John Landy, Australia; Roger Bannister, England) were running mile times which indicated that the sub-4-minute mile was again in jeopardy. In fact, Bannister was so certain the record would shortly fall that he accelerated his workout and racing schedule to make sure that he would have the first good crack at the record. On a cold blustery day in Oxford, not perfect miling conditions by any means, Bannister followed the pacing of Chris Brasher and Chris Chataway for the first three laps, then sprinted the last quarter to break the tape in 3:59.4 — an achievement that is generally considered the most significant in modern track history.

---

* This time is occasionally given as 4:12.75. That can be misleading, however, since it has become convention that only fully automatic times are written to two decimal places. (See "Timing" in the Glossary.) When George ran his record, one-fourth of a second was the smallest amount watches could measure.

Bannister's haste to get the record first was warranted, since John Landy ran 3:57.9 only a few weeks later. In the thirty years that have passed, the track world has seen hundreds of sub-4-minute miles, with two great milers, John Walker and Steve Scott, each having more than a hundred.

When U.S. high school runner Jim Ryun broke 4 minutes in 1964, it was predicted that soon many of the best high school middle-distance runners would be able to run comparable times. However, in the twenty-two years since Ryun's record was set, only two other high school runners have run a mile in less than 4 minutes. This fact highlights another aspect of 4-minute-mile training. Even though almost commonplace at major track events, the 4-minute mile still represents a formidable challenge for even the most talented. The foundation needed takes years to establish, even by the elite runners who have been successful in achieving that goal.

## A Word on Talent

While writing this book — and throughout our coaching careers — we have endeavored to simplify complicated training and racing concepts and have introduced sets of time standards which, once attained, indicate that the runner is ready to begin training for a specific time at a specific distance. As we pointed out in our first book, these standards work successfully for the majority of runners; but there were some who were unable to run the standards yet nonetheless could achieve the time goal in competition. Similarly, there are runners who are able to achieve the recommended pre-training times yet who will fail to achieve the time goal for the specific goal distance. It is becoming increasingly apparent that as the percentage of participants in running increases — and as coaching knowledge improves — a wider variety of physiological types can have success at given distances.

We can see this "subgroup" phenomenon among the runners who have been successful at training for and racing the 4-minute mile. A number of runners have attained the suggested speed standards (220 yards in 23.8 seconds, 440 yards in 52.0), but have been unsuccessful in their attempt to break 4 minutes. Empirical observation suggests that the smaller the margin by which the runner exceeds the standards, the more high-mileage training is required and the more the runner must build miling speed through overall running strength.

Milers who, on the other hand, have the gift of tremendous inherent speed (sub-22-second 220; sub-50-second 440) have been known to run 4-minute miles on as little training as 30 miles a week. Even for these runners, however, higher mileage will be required before they reach their full potential. The miling superstars of recent track history possess blistering speed and combine that with fairly heavy training. Herb Elliott often ran beyond the marathon distance in his miling preparation; Peter Snell, although an Olympic gold medalist in the 800-meter and 1,500-meter runs, occasionally raced a marathon. Steve Ovett has raced half-marathons (13.1 miles), and current 1,500-meter world-record holder Said Aouita is a long-distance specialist, with both the world record and an Olympic gold medal at 5,000 meters.

## Attempt at 4 Minutes

The runner we have chosen to illustrate the development of a 4-minute miler is Len Hilton, former U.S. mile champion and U.S. Olympic representative. Hilton is a good choice for several reasons:

• His best high school time (4:15) places him in the category of promising but not super-talented, and thus his experiences are more applicable to very good, but not great, runners. Similarly, he was able to achieve the 220 and 440 standards required, but not by a wide margin, so it was essential for him to adopt the "mileage training ethic" in his attempt to become a sub-4-minute miler and to build his speed through strength.

• It took Hilton three years to build a sufficient base for his assault on 4 minutes, and during this period he suffered a series of injuries that threatened to end his career. The three-year background period is not unusual for moderately talented high school milers, and his ability to overcome injuries demonstrates that perseverance is just as important in overcoming setbacks as it is in training itself.

• Once Hilton broke through 4 minutes, his training provided him with a base which enabled him to repeat that level of performance (sub-4:00 for a mile or sub-3:42 for 1,500 meters) thirty-one more times in his career.

We pick up Len Hilton's training in October of 1972, as he prepares the foundation of what will be his most important track season to date. This is the third year of his serious training for the mile; his previous two winters had schedules similar to the one given below. However, this season Hilton brings added maturity and a significant mileage base (acquired over the previous two years) to his training, and he has built in a strong acceleration through several years of "speed through the back door" training (see Glossary). His goal is to win the national mile championship. To do so, Hilton is certain he will need to break 4 minutes by several seconds.

To give potential milers a taste of the winter preparation of a sub-4-minute miler, we have abstracted the essential elements of Hilton's less specialized training, which led up to the final eighteen-week program before his season peak. In the following schedules, "easy running" is 6:00 to 6:30 per mile. (Additionally, Hilton divided his mileage into two-a-day training sessions.)

## *October*

| | |
|---|---|
| Total mileage: | 342 |
| Longest run: | 17 miles |
| Rest days: | 3 |
| Strength runs: | 3 (6 miles in 34:56, 31:45, 30:52) |
| Track workouts: | 3 • 10 × 440 in :70; 220 R |
| | • 2 × 1½ miles in 6:50; 880 R |
| | • 3 × 660 in 1:40; 220 R |

## *November*

| | |
|---|---|
| Total mileage: | 401 |
| Longest run: | 19 miles |
| Rest days: | 2 |
| Strength runs: | 4 (6 miles in 35:07, 34:56, 34:26; 3 miles in 14:23) |
| Track workouts: | 6 • 5 × 440 in :68, 440 R; jog 1 mile; 2 × 1 mile in 4:50; 440 R |
| | • 4 × ¾ mile in 3:35, 3:29, 3:29, 3:29; 440 R |
| | • 1 × 880 in 1:55; 6:00 rest; 1 × 660 in 1:26 |
| | • 1 × 2 miles in 9:05; 6:00 rest; 2 × 550 (440 clockings :55 and :57); 660 R |
| | • 5 × 880 in 2:23, 2:20, 2:20, 2:18, 2:13; 440 R |
| | • 3 × 330 in :42, :45, :46; 110 R; 6:00 rest; 8 × 110 in :13; 330 R |

## December

Total mileage:    378
Longest run:      16
Rest days:        0
Strength runs:    4  (6 miles in 34:06, 33:36, 33:13; 4 miles in 22:16)
Track workouts:   5  • 4 × 440 in :59, :59, :59, :60; 220 R; jog 1 mile; 4 × 330 in :44, :44, :44, :43; 110 R
                     • 2 × 1½ miles in 6:59; 880 R
                     • ¾ mile in 3:08; 440 R; 880 in 2:14; 440 R; 440 in :57; 660 R; 220 in :27
                     • 2 miles in 9:40; jog 1 mile; 2 × 110 in :12.5; 220 R; jog 440; 220 in :25
                     • 2 × 1 mile in 4:17, 4:27; 440 R; jog 880; 2 × 220 in :25.5, :26; 660 R
Competitions:     3  • 2 miles in 8:42.4
                     • 2 miles in 8:42.6
                     • 1 mile in 4:06.6

## January

Total mileage:    418
Longest run:      18 miles
Rest days:        1
Strength runs:    3  (6 miles in 35:33, 34:45; 4 miles in 24:03)
Track workouts:   13 • 20 × 220 in :33.5; 220 R
                     • 20 × 330 in :52; 110 R
                     • ¾ mile in 3:17; 12:00 R; 2 × 550 (440 clockings :56, :58); 880 R
                     • 4 × ¾ mile in 3:35; 440 R
                     • 3 × 440 in :60, :61, :63; 220 R; jog 1 mile; 3 × 330 in :44, :44, :45; 110 R; jog 880; 3 × 220 in :28; 440 R
                     • 12 × 110 in :13.5; 330 R
                     • 8 × 220 in :34; 110 R
                     • 1 mile in 4:19; 880 R; 2 × 220 in :25.5, :26; 660 R
                     • 3 × 1½ miles in 7:09, 7:09, 7:15; 880 R
                     • 3 × 550 (440 clockings :56, :56, :58); 330 R
                     • 3 × ¾ mile in 3:14.5, 3:19, 3:20.5; 440 R
                     • 20 × 440 in :67; 220 R
                     • 6 × 220 in :30; 220 R; jog 880; 3 × 220 in :27; 440 R

During the conditioning phases covered in the last several months, most of the rest days were necessitated by upper respiratory infections, treated with aspirin and, in the case of secondary infections, with antibiotics. In the *specialized training* that follows, we begin with February 1, 1973.

## 1st Week

*Day*

1   12 miles easy running incorporating 6 × 220 in :31

2   A.M. 6 miles easy running with 8 × 100 (fast and controlled)
P.M. 6 miles easy running

3   Competition: First in 2-mile race — 8:53.0; first in 1-mile race — 4:16.0

4   A.M. 12 miles easy running
P.M. 8 miles easy running

5   11 miles easy running incorporating 6 × 880 in 2:15; 440 R

6   A.M. 6 miles easy running
P.M. 16 miles easy running incorporating 10 miles in 56:16

7   10 miles easy running on track incorporating 3 × 550 (440 clockings :53.5, :54.5, :57); 880 R

## 2nd Week

*Day*

1   10 miles easy running

2   A.M. 4 miles easy running with 6 × 100 (fast and controlled)
P.M. 6 miles easy running

3   A.M. 3 miles easy running
P.M. Competition: Last in 2-mile race — 8:46.7

4   A.M. 15 miles easy running
P.M. 8 miles easy running

5   14 miles easy running incorporating 3 × 1½ miles in 7:03, 7:01, 6:59; 4:00 R

6   4 miles easy running

7   8 miles easy running incorporating 4 × 220 in :27.5

## 3rd Week

*Day*

1   10 miles easy running

2   A.M. 2 miles easy running
P.M. Competition: Second in 1-mile race — 4:03.2

3   10 miles easy running

4   A.M. 11 miles easy running with 6 × 110 (fast and controlled)
P.M. 9 miles easy running incorporating 2 × 1 mile in 4:16.5, 4:26.5; 440 R; 4 × 220 in :29; 440 R

5   10 × 220 in 32; 220 R; jog 880; 10 × 220 in :32; 220 R

6   3 × 550 (440 clockings :54.3, :54.9, :55.3); 880 R; jog 2 miles; 4 miles in 22:38

7   7 miles easy running

## 4th Week

*Day*

1   8 miles easy running

2   A.M. 4 miles easy running
P.M. Competition: 3-mile race (did not finish)

3   Rest day

4   4 miles easy running

5   Rest day

6   10 miles easy running incorporating 4 × 220 in :33

7   9 miles easy running incorporating 4 × 220 in :30; 440 R; jog 880; 3 × 220 in :25.5; 660 R

## 5th Week

*Day*

1   10 miles easy running

2   6 miles easy running

3   A.M. 2 miles easy running
P.M. Competition: Sixth in 1-mile race — 4:05.8

4   A.M. 16 miles easy running
P.M. 8 miles easy running

5   10 miles easy running

6   13 miles easy running incorporating 12 × 110 in :13; 330 R; 4 miles in 22:04

7   3 × 440 in :57; 110 R; jog 660; 1 × 880 in 2:01

## 6th Week

*Day*

1   10 × 440 in :67; 220 R; jog 880; 10 × 440 in :67; 220 R

2   A.M. 6 miles easy running with 10 × 100 (fast and controlled) P.M. 8 miles easy running

3   4 × 220 in :29; 440 R; jog 880; 1 × 880 in 1:56.5; jog 880; 2 × 220 in :25.5; 660 R

4   6 miles easy running

5   A.M. 16 miles easy running P.M. 6 miles easy running with 8 × 60 (fast and controlled)

6   4 × 330 in :43; 110 R; jog 1 mile; 3 × 110 in :41.5; 110 R

7   10 miles easy running incorporating 4 miles in 22:03

## 7th Week

*Day*

1   7 miles easy running

2   3 × 660 in 1:28; 880 R; jog 880; 4 × 220 in :25.5; 660 R

3   10 miles easy running

4   A.M. 15 miles easy running P.M. 6 miles easy running with 10 × 100 (fast and controlled)

5   A.M. 14 miles easy running P.M. 4 miles easy running incorporating 2 × 220 in :28.5 and 1 × 440 in :54

6   3 × 1½ miles in 6:57, 6:54, 6:58; 880 R

7   2 × 110 in :12.5, 12; 330 R; jog 440; 3 × 440 in :60.5; 220 R; 330 in :40.5; jog 440; 110 in :12.5; jog 2 miles; 2 miles in 11:25

## 8th Week

*Day*

1   7 miles easy running with 5 × 100 (fast and controlled)

2   10 miles easy running

3   4 miles easy running incorporating 1 × ¾ mile in 3:12

4   A.M. 6 miles easy running P.M. Competition: 880 — 1:54.4 (relay leg); first in 1-mile race — 4:16.7

5   16 miles easy running

6   4 × ¾ mile in 3:30, 3:28, 3:26, 3:25; 440 R

7   3 × 550 (440 clocking :55); 880 R; jog 2 miles; 4 miles in 23:00

## 9th Week

*Day*

1   5 miles easy running

2   12 miles easy running

3   6 miles easy running

4   A.M. 3 miles easy running P.M. Competition: First in 1-mile race — 3:58.5 (Florida Relays)

5   A.M. 10 miles easy running P.M. 8 miles easy running

6   10 miles easy running

7   9 miles easy running incorporating 12 × 110 in :13

## 10th Week

*Day*

1   3 miles easy running incorporating 4 × 220 in :25.5

2   A.M. 6 miles easy running incorporating 10 × 110 (fast and controlled) P.M. 3 × 880 in 2:19, 2:18, 2:19; 440 R

3   10 miles easy running

4   A.M. 6 miles easy running with 8 × 100 (fast and controlled) P.M. Competition: First in 880 race — 1:51.2; first in 3-mile race — 14:07.8

5   19 miles easy running

6   3 × 1 mile in 4:36; 440 R

7  2 × 550 (440 clocking :55.5);
   440 R; jog 2 miles; 4 miles in
   21:13

## 11th Week

*Day*

1  A.M. 6 miles easy running with
   10 × 80 (fast and controlled)
   P.M. 2 × 220 in :27; 440 R; jog
   880; 3 × 330 in :45; 220 R
2  10 miles easy running
3  8 miles easy running
4  A.M. 3 miles easy running
   P.M. Competition: Eighth in 1-
   mile race — 4:02.9
5  A.M. 11 miles easy running
   P.M. 6 miles easy running with
   8 × 110 (fast and controlled)
6  10 miles easy running
7  A.M. 6 miles easy running with
   8 × 110 (fast and controlled)
   P.M. 2 × 880 in 1:54; 1¼ miles
   R; jog 2 miles; 4 miles in 23:00

## 12th Week

*Day*

1  8 miles easy running with
   8 × 110 in :13.5
2  12 miles easy running
3  7 miles easy running
4  A.M. 3 miles easy running
   P.M. Competition: First in 1-
   mile race — 4:01.9 (Kansas
   Relays)
5  20 miles easy running
6  2 × 1½ miles in 7:10; 880 R
7  A.M. 6 miles easy running with
   8 × 110 (fast and controlled)
   P.M. ¾ mile in 3:03; jog 1 mile;
   3 × 220 in :25; 440 R; jog 2
   miles; 2 miles in 11:30

## 13th Week

*Day*

1  440 in :57; 440 R; 3 × 110 in
   :13; 330 R; jog 880; 880 in 2:07

2  12 miles easy running
3  8 miles easy running
4  A.M. 3 miles easy running
   P.M. Competition: 1 mile —
   4:04.9 (relay)
5  10 miles easy running
6  10 × 440 in :65; 440 R; jog 880;
   8 × 440 in :66; 220 R
7  6 miles easy running

## 14th Week

*Day*

1  3 miles easy running
2  13 miles easy running incorporating 12 × 110 in :13 and 4
   miles in 21:30
3  A.M. 6 miles easy running with
   8 × 110 (fast and controlled)
   P.M. 10 miles easy running
4  A.M. 2 × 1 mile in 4:11; 1 mile
   R; jog 2 miles; 330 in :46; 220
   in :30; 3 × 110 in :13; all 220 R
   P.M. 15 miles easy running
5  A.M. 12 miles easy running
   P.M. 6 miles easy running with
   8 × 60 (fast and controlled)
6  2 × ¾ mile in 3:30; 440 R
7  1 × 550 (440 clocking :52); jog
   880; 1 × 440 in :54.5; jog 880; 3
   miles in 17:00

## 15th Week

*Day*

1  Rest day
2  10 miles easy running
3  8 miles easy running
4  A.M. 2 miles easy running
   P.M. Competition: First in 1-
   mile race — 4:05.7; first in 3-
   mile race — 13:55.8
5  10 miles easy running
6  4 × 1 mile in 4:52; 220 R
7  10 miles easy running incorporating 6 miles in 32:36

*Hilton's championship season was punctuated by this close win over Randy Melancon of the New York Athletic Club in the Gulf Amateur Athletic Union 3-Mile Championship. (Photograph copyright © Houston Chronicle)*

## 16th Week

*Day*

1   12 miles easy running
2   5 × 880 in 2:16; 220 R; jog 880; 1 × 660 in 1:30
3   10 miles easy running
4   A.M. 2 × 220 in :28; 440 R; jog 1 mile; 2 × 660 in 1:22; 1 mile R
    P.M. 14 miles easy running
5   17 miles easy running incorporating 3 miles in 15:00
6   12 miles easy running with 12 × 100 (fast and controlled)
7   A.M. 6 miles easy running with 8 × 150 (fast and controlled)
    P.M. 2 × 550 (440 clocking :55); 110 R; jog 1 mile; 4 miles in 23:40

## 17th Week

*Day*

1   8 miles easy running
2   A.M. 6 miles easy running incorporating 10 × 100 (fast and controlled)
    P.M. 3 × 220 in :26; 440 R
3   10 miles easy running
4   A.M. 4 miles easy running incorporating 6 × 100 (fast and controlled)
    P.M. 3 miles easy running
5   A.M. 2 miles easy running
    P.M. Competition: 1-mile race — 4:01.4 (unplaced)
6   6 miles easy running
7   4 × 440 in :58; 220 R; jog ¾ mile; 4 × 330 in :43.5; 110 R

## 18th Week

*Day*

1   6 miles easy running incorporating 10 × 100 (fast and controlled)
2   8 miles easy running
3   A.M. 4 miles easy running
    P.M. 3 miles easy running
4   A.M. 2 miles easy running
    P.M. Competition: Seventh in 880 race — 1:51.4; second in 3-mile race — 13:50.5
5   Rest day
6   9 miles easy running
7   4 miles easy running incorporating 2 × 880 in 2:20

## 19th Week

*Day*

1   6 × 550 (440 clocking averaging :58.2); 110 R; jog 1 mile; 880 in 1:56
2   12 miles easy running incorporating 6 miles in 32:55
3   A.M. 6 miles easy running incorporating 6 × 110 (fast and controlled)
    P.M. 10 miles easy running
4   A.M. 10 miles easy running
    P.M. ¾ mile in 3:04; 880 R; 1½ miles in 7:00
5   A.M. 12 miles easy running
    P.M. 8 miles easy running incorporating 10 × 100 (fast and controlled)
6   Rest day
7   10 miles easy running

## 20th Week

*Day*

1   8 miles easy running
2   A.M. 2 miles easy running
    P.M. Competition: First in 1-mile race — 4:00.5 (heat of U.S. National Championships)
3   A.M. 5 miles easy running
    P.M. 3 miles easy running incorporating 4 × 100 (fast and controlled)
4   A.M. 2 miles easy running
    P.M. Competition: *First in 1-mile race — 3:55.9* (finals, U.S. National Championships)

In the long saga of Len Hilton's preparation to win a national championship, two points are of interest to an aspiring elite miler. The first is the tremendous quality and quantity of work Hilton needed to do to achieve his goals. We have touched on this point several times, but it is perhaps more vivid when a prospective runner can see the actual workouts and imagine, from his or her own experience, the dedication necessary to run a hard track workout in the morning and follow that with a long run in the afternoon, bringing the average daily mileage up to that of many marathoners.

The second point is the erratic nature of Len's racing during the spring season leading to his national championship. Aside from the one sub-4-minute effort that won the Florida Relays in the ninth week of his specialized training, his efforts were marked either by wins in easy mile races around 4:05 or nonwinning efforts just over 4 minutes. Len and I began to wonder whether he had peaked at Gainesville and was not going to be seriously competitive again that season. As the national championships neared, we knew that he was continuing to train well, but we were no closer to knowing from his races whether he was in national-level racing form. To discover whether there was anything extra left, we devised the workout Len ran on Day 1 of the nineteenth week of training. After he had demonstrated that he could run repeat 550s at sub-4-minute pace with a minimal recovery (110 yards) and then — after a mile jog — run a 1:56 half-mile, we knew that the ability was still there and that he could approach the nationals with the idea that he had not yet tapped his full potential. (See the full discussion on benchmark workouts in Chapter 2.)

*David Reinhart (leading David Edge), independent sales representative. (Photograph by Connie S. Butler / Brooks Shoe Inc.)*

# The 4:15 Mile or 3:56 1,500 Meters

> *You are ready to train for a 4:15 mile if you can run:*
>
> *220 yards in 26 seconds*
> *440 yards in 55.5 seconds*
>
> *To run a 4:15 mile, you will need to average 63.75 seconds per quarter*

The 4:15 mile is the province of a select group of runners. Male high school runners who attain this standard will be ranked in the top ten in the nation and thus will be eagerly sought out by college coaches, who are aware that most such young runners, given the proper coaching and training, can make a 10- to 20-second improvement in their mile times during their four-year college career.

Women who can run this time or the equivalent metrical clocking can be classified as among the top two or three female middle-distance runners in the world. A male master's runner (forty years and older) who can run 4:15 is among the super-elite at the national or international level.

Although among male collegiate runners a 4:15 mile is nothing to write home about, the time is significant for specialists in distance races and cross-country, whose attainment of this standard provides a strong speed base for the longer events and the reasonable expectation that as they lower their mile time they can run even faster over longer distances.

A note of caution is in order here: There will be a number of teenage runners who can run the suggested pre-training qualifying standards (220 yards in 26 seconds, 440 yards in 55.5) with ease but cannot approach the mile target time. Coaches and runners should be aware that speed without the necessary "strength" (which here means short-distance endurance) will not produce good mile times. This strength is generally a product of physical and physiological maturity, and the time at which it becomes manifest is hard to predict. Teenage endurance runners develop at their own pace, and the early years of training should be largely directed to developing general strength and a running foundation.

In the following schedules, "easy running" is 6:30 to 7:00 per mile. "R" means jog recovery unless otherwise specified; when "R" represents a time, the interval should be spent walking or resting.

*PRE-CONDITIONING*

The period before specialized training begins should be eight weeks long. The recommended mileage is 40 to 60 miles per week. Each track workout should begin with a 1- to 2-mile easy warm-up and end with a 1- to 2-mile easy warm-down.

*Phase 1.* Four weeks:

*Day*

| | | | |
|---|---|---|---|
| 1 | 8–10 miles easy running | 16 | 12 × 220 in :32; 220 walk R |
| 2 | 16 × 110 in :17; 110 walk R | 17 | 7 miles easy running incorporating 2 miles in 10:00 |
| 3 | 4 × 440 in :68; 220 walk R | | |
| 4 | 8 miles easy running | 18 | 6 miles easy running |
| 5 | 2 miles in 10:30 | 19 | 12 × 440 in :70; 220 walk R |
| 6 | 12 × 110 in :15; 110 walk R | 20 | 6 miles easy running |
| 7 | 7 miles in 42:00 | 21 | 8 miles in 48:00 |
| 8 | 10 miles easy running | 22 | 20 × 110 in :15; 110 jog R |
| 9 | 16 × 110 in :15; 110 walk R | 23 | 6 miles easy running |
| 10 | 6 miles easy running | 24 | 6 × 660 in 1:45; 440 jog R |
| 11 | 4 × 660 in 1:45; 440 walk R | 25 | 4 miles easy running |
| 12 | 10 miles easy running | 26 | 12 × 110 in :14; 220 jog R |
| 13 | 8 miles in 48:00 | 27 | 6 miles easy running |
| 14 | 8 miles easy running | 28 | 10 miles easy running |
| 15 | 10 miles easy running | | |

*Phase 2.* Four weeks consisting of two times the following fourteen-day training schedule:

*Day*

| | | | |
|---|---|---|---|
| 1 | 6 miles in 34:30 | 8 | 8 miles easy running |
| 2 | 440 in :68; jog 110; 110 in :14; jog 440 — repeat set 5 more times | 9 | 880 in 2:10; 440 in :60; 220 in :28; all 660 R |
| 3 | 8 miles easy running | 10 | 6 miles easy running |
| 4 | 16 × 110 in :14; 110 R | 11 | 12 × 110 in :14; 330 R |
| 5 | 8 miles easy running | 12 | 8 miles easy running |
| 6 | Rest day | 13 | Rest day |
| 7 | 12 miles in 76:00 | 14 | 10 miles in 57:30 |

*SPECIALIZED TRAINING*

You are now ready to begin the final six weeks of sharpening training leading to your attempt on the 4:15-mile mark.

## 1st Week

*Day*

1  10 miles easy running
2  880 in 2:08; 440 in :60; 220 in :28; all 660 R
3  6 miles easy running
4  8 × 110 in :13.5; 220 R; rest 5:00; 8 x 110 in :13.5; 220 R
5  3 miles easy running
6  5 miles easy running incorporating 2 × 1 mile in 4:50
7  8 miles easy running

## 2nd Week

*Day*

1  6 miles in 34:30
2  660 in 1:40; 110 R; 110 in :14; 550 R — repeat set 3 more times
3  6 miles easy running
4  4 miles easy running
5  4 × 220 in :29; 440 R; rest 5:00; 880 time trial
6  4 miles easy running
7  8 miles in 48:00

## 3rd Week

*Day*

1  6 miles easy running incorporating 2 miles in 10:00
2  12 × 220 in :32; 220 R
3  5 miles easy running
4  ¾ mile in 3:20; 660 R; 880 in 2:08
5  6 miles easy running

6  440 in :66; 110 R; 110 in :14; 440 R — repeat set 5 more times
7  4 miles easy running

## 4th Week

*Day*

1  10 miles in 60:00
2  3 × 880 in 2:15; 660 R
3  6 miles easy running
4  2 miles in 9:40
5  6 miles easy running
6  Rest day
7  2 × ¾ mile in 3:14; ¾ mile R

## 5th Week

*Day*

1  8 miles easy running
2  10 × 440 in :68; 440 R
3  4 miles easy running
4  ¾ mile in 3:12; 10:00 rest; 1 × 880 in 2:07
5  6 miles easy running
6  10 × 110 in :13; 330 R
7  8 miles easy running

## 6th Week

*Day*

1  6 miles in 35:00
2  6 × 440 in :62; 440 R
3  5 miles easy running
4  12 × 110 in :15; 110 R
5  Rest day
6  3 miles easy running
7  Mile race in 4:15

*Rene Odom, office manager. (Photograph by Conrad J. McCarthy)*

# The 4:30 Mile or 4:10 1,500 Meters

*You are ready to train for a 4:30 mile if you can run:*

*220 yards in 27 seconds*
*440 yards in 58.5 seconds*

*To run a 4:30 mile, you will need to average 67.5 seconds per quarter*

The 4:30 mile represents a significant achievement to a number of different middle-distance athletes. It serves as the threshold for a male high school runner who hopes to win a major college track scholarship. At the male master's level (over forty) it marks the competitor as one of national caliber. For women, the 4:30 mile is the watershed standard that marks the runner as world class, worthy to represent her country in international competition.

As in the other schedules for this distance, we presume that the runner may be coming off a busy winter and early spring distance program and will want to modify the pre-conditioning program by taking a little longer and easing into the more intense track work. On the other hand, some runners, especially high schoolers, may have competed in the indoor season and already reached one mile peak, and so will not require as much pre-conditioning after they have completed their post-season recovery.

### PRE-CONDITIONING

The pre-conditioning period before the 4:30 mile is attempted in the outdoor season should be six to eight weeks. You should be running 35 to 50 miles per week. Each track workout should begin with a 1- to 2-mile easy warm-up and end with a 1- to 2-mile easy warm-down. "Easy running" in this schedule is 7:00 to 7:45 per mile. "R" means jog recovery unless otherwise specified; when "R" represents a time, the interval should be spent walking or resting.

*Phase 1.* The first two weeks:

Day

1   4–6 miles easy running
2   16 × 110 in :18; 110 walk back R
3   4 × 440 in :75; 220 walk R
4   6 miles easy running
5   2 miles in 11:30
6   12 × 110 in :16; 110 walk R
7   5 miles in 30:00
8   9 miles easy running
9   16 × 110 in :16; 110 R
10   3 miles easy running
11   4 × 660 in 1:52; 440 walk R
12   5 miles easy running
13   6 miles in 36:00
14   8 miles easy running

*Phase 2.* The second two weeks:

Day

1   9 miles easy running
2   12 × 220 in :35; 220 walk R
3   5 miles easy running incorporating 2 miles in 11:00
4   6 miles easy running
5   12 × 440 in :75; 220 walk R
6   5 miles easy running
7   7 miles in 42:00
8   20 × 110 in :17; 110 jog R
9   6 miles easy running
10   6 × 660 in 1:52; 440 R
11   3 miles easy running
12   12 × 110 in :15; 220 jog R
13   5 miles easy running
14   9 miles easy running

*Phase 3.* The following seven-day program should be repeated until the runner feels prepared to move on to the final six weeks of specialized training. If the runner feels ready, he or she should spend only one week in Phase 3; up to four weeks may be taken if that seems necessary.

Day

1   5 miles in 29:00
2   440 in :72; jog 110; 110 in :15; 440 R — repeat set 5 more times
3   6 miles easy running
4   16 × 110 in :15; 110 jog R
5   6 miles easy running
6   Rest day
7   10 miles in 70:00

SPECIALIZED TRAINING

The final six weeks of training leading up to the 4:30 mile:

*1st Week*

Day

1   7 miles easy running
2   880 in 2:20; 440 in :66; 220 in :31; all 660 R
3   5 miles easy running
4   8 × 110 in :14.5; 220 R; rest 5:00; 8 × 110 in :14.5; 220 R
5   3 miles easy running
6   4 miles easy running incorporating 2 × 1 mile in 5:10
7   6 miles easy running

## 2nd Week

### Day

1   6 miles in 36:00
2   660 in 1:45; 110 R; 110 in :15; 550 R — repeat set 3 more times
3   5 miles easy running
4   3 miles easy running
5   4 × 220 in :32; 440 R; 5:00 rest; 880 time trial
6   3 miles easy running
7   7 miles in 42:00

## 3rd Week

### Day

1   5 miles easy running incorporating 2 miles in 11:00
2   12 × 220 in :34; 220 R
3   4 miles easy running
4   ¾ mile (1,320 yards) in 3:36; 660 R; 880 in 2:18
5   6 miles easy running
6   440 in :72; 110 R; 110 in :15; 440 R — repeat set 5 more times
7   3 miles easy running

## 4th Week

### Day

1   10 miles in 65:00
2   3 × 880 in 2:24; 660 R
3   5 miles easy running
4   1½ miles in 7:30
5   5 miles easy running
6   Rest day
7   2 × ¾ mile in 3:28; ¾ mile R

## 5th Week

### Day

1   6 miles easy running
2   10 × 440 in :70; 440 R
3   3 miles easy running
4   ¾ mile in 3:22.5; 10:00 R; 880 in 2:15
5   5 miles easy running
6   8 × 110 in :14; 330 R
7   6 miles easy running

## 6th Week

### Day

1   6 miles in 36:00
2   4 × 440 in :66; 440 walk R
3   4 miles easy running
4   12 × 110 in :16; 110 R
5   Rest day
6   2 miles easy running
7   Mile race in 4:30

*Bruce Glikin, independent businessman. (Photograph by Paul Glikin)*

# The 4:45 Mile or 4:22 1,500 Meters

*You are ready to train for a 4:45 mile if you can run:*

*220 yards in 28.5 seconds*
*440 yards in 61.5 seconds*

*To run a mile in 4:45, you will need to average 71.25 seconds per quarter*

The 4:45 mile is an eagerly sought mark for female high school runners who wish to move into the elite class at state and national levels. Master's men (over forty) who attain this standard are capable of placing in national championship meets. High school cross-country and track distance runners know that this type of miling speed — when coupled with their long-distance endurance — will allow them to make the school team in their longer specialties.

### PRE-CONDITIONING

Before attempting to run a 4:45 mile during the outdoor season, you should plan on a pre-race conditioning phase of six weeks, with weekly mileage in the 35-to-45 range. Each track workout should begin with a 1- to 2-mile easy warm-up and end with a 1- to 2-mile easy warm-down. "Easy running" in this schedule is 7:30 to 8:00 per mile. "R" means jog recovery unless otherwise specified; when "R" represents a time, the interval should be spent walking or resting.

*Phase 1.* The first three weeks:
### Day

| | | | |
|---|---|---|---|
| 1 | 6 miles easy running | 12 | 5 miles easy running |
| 2 | 12 × 110 in :18; 110 walk R | 13 | 6 miles in 37:00 |
| 3 | 4 × 440 in :78; 220 walk R | 14 | 8 miles easy running |
| 4 | 5 miles easy running | 15 | 8 miles easy running |
| 5 | 2 miles in 12:00 | 16 | 10 × 220 in :36; 220 walk R |
| 6 | 12 × 110 in :17; 110 walk R | 17 | 5 miles easy running incorporating 2 miles in 11:30 |
| 7 | 5 miles in 31:00 | | |
| 8 | 8 miles easy running | 18 | 5 miles easy running |
| 9 | 16 × 110 in :17; 110 walk R | 19 | 10 × 440 in :75; 220 walk R |
| 10 | 3 miles easy running | 20 | 5 miles easy running |
| 11 | 4 × 660 in 1:56; 440 walk R | 21 | 7 miles in 43:10 |

*Phase 2.* The second three weeks:

*Day*

| | | | |
|---|---|---|---|
| 1 | 20 × 110 in :18; 110 jog R | 11 | 16 × 110 in :16; 110 jog R |
| 2 | 5 miles easy running | 12 | 5 miles easy running |
| 3 | 5 × 660 in 1:52; 440 jog R | 13 | Rest day |
| 4 | 3 miles easy running | 14 | 8 miles in 56:00 |
| 5 | 12 × 110 in :16; 220 jog R | 15 | 8 miles easy running |
| 6 | 5 miles easy running | 16 | 12 × 110 in :15; 110 jog R |
| 7 | 9 miles easy running | 17 | 6 miles easy running |
| 8 | 5 miles in 30:00 | 18 | 5 miles in 30:00 |
| 9 | 440 in :75; jog 110; 110 in :16; 440 R — repeat set 5 more times | 19 | 6 miles easy running |
| | | 20 | 12 × 220 in :35; 220 jog R |
| 10 | 5 miles easy running | 21 | 8 miles easy running |

### SPECIALIZED TRAINING

You are now prepared to proceed with the final six weeks of specialized training leading to the goal of a 4:45 mile.

## 1st Week

*Day*

1  5 miles easy running
2  880 in 2:25; 440 in :68; 220 in :32; all 660 R
3  5 miles easy running
4  8 × 110 in :15; 220 R; 5:00 rest; 8 × 110 in :15; 220 R
5  3 miles easy running
6  4 miles easy running incorporating 2 × 1 mile in 5:20
7  6 miles easy running

## 2nd Week

*Day*

1  6 miles in 37:00
2  660 in 1:50; 110 in :16; 550 R — repeat set 3 more times
3  5 miles easy running
4  3 miles easy running
5  4 × 220 in :34; 440 R; 5:00 rest; 880 time trial

6  3 miles easy running
7  7 miles in 43:10

## 3rd Week

*Day*

1  5 miles easy running incorporating 2 miles in 11:30
2  10 × 220 in :34; 220 R
3  4 miles easy running
4  ¾ mile in 3:45; 660 R; 880 in 2:25
5  6 miles easy running
6  440 in :74; 110 R; 110 in :16; 440 R — repeat set 5 more times
7  3 miles easy running

## 4th Week

*Day*

1  10 miles in 67:30
2  3 × 880 in 2:30; 660 R
3  5 miles easy running

4   1½ miles in 7:50
5   5 miles easy running
6   Rest day
7   2 × ¾ mile in 3:45; ¾ mile R

## 5th Week

*Day*

1   6 miles easy running
2   10 × 440 in :72; 440 R
3   3 miles easy running
4   ¾ mile in 3:34; 10:00 rest; 880 in 2:22.5
5   5 miles easy running

6   8 × 110 in :14; 330 R
7   6 miles easy running

## 6th Week

*Day*

1   6 miles in 37:00
2   4 × 440 in :68; 440 walk R
3   4 miles easy running
4   12 × 110 in :16.5; 110 R
5   Rest day
6   2 miles easy running
7   Mile race in 4:45

*Debbie Warner, independent businesswoman. (Photograph by Conrad J. McCarthy)*

# The 5:00 Mile or 4:37 1,500 Meters

*You are ready to train for a 5:00 mile if you can run:*

*220 yards in 29.5 seconds*
*440 yards in 64 seconds*

*To run a 5:00 mile, you will need to average 75 seconds per quarter*

There are certain barriers in middle-distance and distance running that represent significant milestones. Elite runners talk of the 2:10 marathon and the 4-minute mile. For the majority of mid-range competitors, the 3-hour marathon is probably the most challenging and exciting barrier in long-distance running. In the intermediate middle distances the same can be said of the 5-minute-mile barrier. Once it is broken, the runner, asked his or her PR in the mile, can truthfully respond, "Oh, four . . . something."

*PRE-CONDITIONING*

A runner planning to run a 5-minute mile should do six to eight weeks of conditioning. If he or she is not racing during this period, the weekly training mileage should be in the range of 30 to 40 miles. Often, a runner preparing for a mile effort will be coming off other training for longer distances, so this mileage can vary greatly and might even be less when this period includes recovery from a marathon or other long effort.

Let's assume that you plan no other racing before your attempt at a 5-minute mile. In that case, we can break the pre-conditioning preparation into three phases, which can be adjusted to fit the time available. Each track workout should begin with a 1- to 2-mile easy warm-up and end with a 1- to 2-mile easy warm-down. In the following schedule, "easy running" is 7:30 to 8:30 per mile. "R" means jog recovery unless otherwise specified; when "R" represents a time, the interval should be spent walking or resting.

*Phase 1.* The first two weeks:

Day

| | | | |
|---|---|---|---|
| 1 | 4–6 miles easy running | 8 | 6–8 miles easy running |
| 2 | 10 × 110 in :19; 110 walk R | 9 | 16 × 110 in :19; 110 walk R |
| 3 | 4 × 440 in :80; 220 walk R | 10 | 3 miles easy running |
| 4 | 4 miles easy running | 11 | 4 × 660 in 2:00; 440 walk R |
| 5 | 2 miles in 12:00 | 12 | 4 miles easy running |
| 6 | 12 × 110 in :19; 110 walk R | 13 | 3 miles in 18:00 |
| 7 | 4 miles in 26:00 | 14 | 6 miles easy running |

*Phase 2.* If you feel you need extra pre-conditioning, this fourteen-day schedule may be repeated for another two weeks:

Day

| | | | |
|---|---|---|---|
| 1 | 6 miles easy running | 8 | 20 × 110 in :19; 110 jog R |
| 2 | 12 × 220 in :39; 220 walk R | 9 | 5 miles easy running |
| 3 | 4 miles easy running incorporating 2 miles in 12:00 | 10 | 6 × 660 in 2:00; 440 jog R |
| | | 11 | 3 miles easy running |
| 4 | 5 miles easy running | 12 | 10 × 110 in :17; 220 jog R |
| 5 | 10 × 440 in :85; 220 walk R | 13 | 4 miles easy running |
| 6 | 5 miles easy running | 14 | 9 miles easy running |
| 7 | 7 miles in 42:00 | | |

*Phase 3.* This is a seven-day series, which can also be repeated at your discretion:

Day

| | | | |
|---|---|---|---|
| 1 | 5 miles in 32:30 | 4 | 16 × 110 in :18; 110 jog R |
| 2 | 440 in :80; 110 jog R; 110 in :17; 440 R — repeat set 5 more times | 5 | 6 miles easy running |
| | | 6 | Rest day |
| | | 7 | 9 miles in 63:00 |
| 3 | 5 miles easy running | | |

## SPECIALIZED TRAINING

The necessary foundation has now been laid, and you are ready to proceed with the final six weeks of specialized training leading to the 5-minute mile.

## 1st Week

*Day*

1  7 miles easy running
2  880 in 2:35; 440 in :74; 220 in :35; all 660 R
3  4 miles easy running
4  8 × 110 in :16; 220 R; 5:00 rest; 8 × 110 in :16; 220 R
5  3 miles easy running
6  4 miles incorporating 2 × 1 mile in 5:30
7  6 miles easy running

## 2nd Week

*Day*

1  5 miles in 32:30
2  660 in 1:52; 110 R; 110 in :16; 550 R — repeat set 3 more times
3  4 miles easy running
4  3 miles easy running
5  4 × 220 in :35; 440 R; 5:00 rest; 880 time trial
6  3 miles easy running
7  7 miles in 45:00

## 3rd Week

*Day*

1  5 miles easy running incorporating 2 miles in 11:45
2  12 × 220 in :36; 220 R
3  4 miles easy running
4  ¾ mile in 4:00; 880 in 2:35; 660 R
5  5 miles easy running
6  440 in :78; 110 R; 110 in :16; 440 R — repeat set 5 more times
7  6 miles easy running

## 4th Week

*Day*

1  9 miles in 63:00
2  3 × 880 in 2:35; 660 R
3  5 miles easy running
4  1½ miles in 8:15
5  4 miles easy running
6  Rest day
7  2 × ¾ mile in 4:00; 880 R

## 5th Week

*Day*

1  9 miles easy running
2  10 × 440 in :78; 440 R
3  4 miles easy running
4  3 miles easy running
5  ¾ mile in 3:45; 10:00 R; 880 in 2:30
6  5 miles easy running
7  6 miles in 38:00

## 6th Week

*Day*

1  6 miles easy running
2  5 × 440 in :72; 440 walk R
3  3 miles easy running
4  12 × 110 in :18; 110 R (Don't run these too fast!)
5  Rest day
6  2 miles easy running
7  Mile race in 5:00

*Shirlie Lindsay, interior designer. (Photograph by Bruce Glikin)*

# The 5:30 Mile or 5:04 1,500 Meters

*You are ready to train for a 5:30 mile if you can run:*

*220 yards in 33.5 seconds*
*440 yards in 72 seconds*

*To run a 5:30 mile, you will need to average 82.5 seconds per quarter*

The 5:30 mile clocking doesn't really serve as a benchmark for any class of runner. Unlike the case with the faster mile times discussed in this book, there is no feeling of "I'm there!" engendered when you break 5:30 for the first time. A 5:30 mile — by itself — won't get you much respect in serious mile competition.

Training for it, however, *will* translate to increased speed in your longer runs and increased endurance in your shorter runs and the long sprints. Even more important, especially for those who are doing serious short-distance training for the first time (probably many readers of this book), the 5:30 mile serves as another barrier to be surmounted as you work toward lowering your mile time toward your personal best. Successfully completing the training for the 5:30 mile will prepare you to begin training for a sub-5-minute mile. And, after all, every world-record holder in the history of the mile, at some point in his or her mile career, had to break 5:30 for the first time. You are merely following in their footsteps.

Two conditioning periods of twenty-one days are recommended before the runner begins the final six-week training period leading to the 5:30 mile. Weekly mileage should average 30 to 40 miles during both the conditioning and the specialized training phases. Each track workout should begin with a 1- to 2-mile easy warm-up and end with a 1- to 2-mile easy warm-down. "Easy running" in this schedule is 7:45 to 8:45 per mile. "R" means jog recovery unless otherwise specified; when "R" represents a time, the interval should be spent walking or resting.

## PRE-CONDITIONING

*Phase 1.* The first twenty-one days:

*Day*

| | | | |
|---|---|---|---|
| 1 | 4 miles easy running | 12 | 4 miles easy running |
| 2 | 10 × 110 in :20; 110 walk R | 13 | 3 miles in 19:30 |
| 3 | 4 × 440 in :85; 220 walk R | 14 | 6 miles easy running |
| 4 | 4 miles easy running | 15 | 6 miles easy running |
| 5 | 2 miles in 13:00 | 16 | 12 × 220 in :42; 220 walk R |
| 6 | 12 × 110 in :20; 110 walk R | 17 | 4 miles easy running incorporating 2 miles in 13:00 |
| 7 | 4 miles in 28:00 | | |
| 8 | 6 miles easy running | 18 | 5 miles easy running |
| 9 | 16 × 110 in :20; 110 walk R | 19 | 10 × 440 in :90; 220 walk R |
| 10 | 3 miles easy running | 20 | 5 miles easy running |
| 11 | 4 × 660 in 2:10; 440 walk R | 21 | 7 miles in 45:00 |

*Phase 2.* The second twenty-one days:

*Day*

| | | | |
|---|---|---|---|
| 1 | 20 × 110 in :20; 110 jog R | 11 | 16 × 110 in :19; 110 jog R |
| 2 | 5 miles easy running | 12 | 6 miles easy running |
| 3 | 6 × 660 in 2:10; 440 jog R | 13 | Rest day |
| 4 | 3 miles easy running | 14 | 8 miles in 60:00 |
| 5 | 10 × 110 in :18; 220 jog R | 15 | 10 × 110 in :18; 330 jog R |
| 6 | 4 miles easy running | 16 | 5 miles easy running |
| 7 | 8 miles easy running | 17 | 3 miles easy running |
| 8 | 5 miles in 35:00 | 18 | 10 × 220 in :38; 440 R |
| 9 | 440 in :85; 110 jog R; 110 in :18; 440 R — repeat set 5 more times | 19 | 6 miles easy running |
| | | 20 | 8 miles easy running |
| 10 | 5 miles easy running | 21 | Rest day |

## SPECIALIZED TRAINING

The final six-week period of specialized training:

*1st Week*

*Day*

| | | | |
|---|---|---|---|
| 1 | 6 miles easy running | 4 | 8 × 110 in :17.5; 220 R; 5:00 rest; 8 × 110 in :17.5; 220 R |
| 2 | 880 in 2:50; 440 in :77; 220 in :37.5; all 660 R | 5 | 3 miles easy running |
| | | 6 | 4 miles easy running incorporating 2 × 1 mile in 6:00 |
| 3 | 4 miles easy running | 7 | 6 miles easy running |

## 2nd Week

*Day*

1. 5 miles in 37:30
2. 660 in 2:00; 110 R; 110 in :18; 550 R — repeat set 3 more times
3. 4 miles easy running
4. 3 miles easy running
5. 4 × 220 in :40; 440 R; 5:00 rest; 880 time trial
6. 3 miles easy running
7. 7 miles in 49:00

## 3rd Week

*Day*

1. 5 miles easy running incorporating 2 miles in 12:30
2. 12 × 220 in :38; 220 R
3. 4 miles easy running
4. ¾ mile in 4:15; 880 in 2:50; 660 R
5. 5 miles easy running
6. 440 in :84; 110 R; 110 in :17; 440 R — repeat set 5 more times
7. 6 miles easy running

## 4th Week

*Day*

1. 8 miles in 58:00
2. 3 × 880 in 2:50; 660 R
3. 5 miles easy running
4. 1½ miles in 9:00
5. 4 miles easy running
6. Rest day
7. 2 × ¾ mile in 4:15; 880 R

## 5th Week

*Day*

1. 8 miles easy running
2. 10 × 440 in :84; 440 R
3. 4 miles easy running
4. 3 miles easy running
5. ¾ mile in 4:07.5; 10:00 rest; 880 in 2:45
6. 5 miles easy running
7. 6 miles in 39:00

## 6th Week

*Day*

1. 6 miles easy running
2. 5 × 440 in :76; 440 walk R
3. 3 miles easy running
4. 12 × 110 in :19; 110 R
5. Rest day
6. 2 miles easy running
7. Mile race in 5:30

*Connie Niehaus, investment banker vice-president. (Photograph by Ronald R. Niehaus)*

# The 6:00 Mile or 5:31 1,500 Meters

*You are ready to train for a 6:00 mile if you can run:*

*220 yards in 37 seconds*
*440 yards in 78 seconds*

*To run a 6:00 mile, you will need to average 90 seconds per quarter*

The U.S. Army once had a run in its physical combat proficiency test. On the army charts, the maximum score (100 points) was awarded to mile times at or under 6 minutes flat. Not very many young men in college ROTC programs could run that fast.

In the world of the self-coached runner, the ability to break 6 minutes for a mile often signals the beginning of serious competitive training for a miler. It is often a satisfying and important challenge, but at times a frustrating one.

Before you start your specialized training for an attempt at the 6-minute-mile barrier, you will need a pre-conditioning phase of six to eight weeks of foundation with mileage in the 25-to-35 range. If you are coming off a road-racing season, six weeks will be enough. Each track workout should begin with a 1- to 2-mile easy warm-up and end with a 1- to 2-mile easy warm-down. In the following schedule, "easy running" is 7:45 to 8:45 per mile. "R" means jog recovery unless otherwise specified; when "R" represents a time, the interval should be spent walking or resting.

## PRE-CONDITIONING

### Phase 1

**Day**

1  3–5 miles easy running
2  10 × 110 in :21; 110 walk R
3  3 × 440 in :92; 220 walk R
4  3 miles easy running
5  2 miles in 14:20
6  8 × 110 in :20; 110 walk R
7  Rest day
8  6 miles easy running

9  12 × 10 in :21; 110 walk R
10  3 miles easy running
11  3 × 660 in 2:25; 440 walk R
12  Rest day
13  3 miles in 22:30
14  5 miles easy running
15  10 × 220 in :43; 220 walk R
16  4 miles easy running incor-

porating 2 miles in 14:00
17   3 miles easy running
18   6 × 440 in :92; 220 walk R

19   4 miles easy running
20   Rest day
21   6 miles in 45:00

## Phase 2

*Day*

1    5 miles easy running
2    12 × 110 in :20; 110 jog R
3    4 miles easy running
4    4 × 660 in 2:25; 440 jog R
5    3 miles easy running
6    Rest day
7    7 miles easy running
8    4 miles in 28:00
9    440 in :90; 110 jog R; 110 in :20; 440 jog R — repeat set 5 more times
10   3 miles easy running
11   10 × 110 in :20; 110 jog R

12   3 miles easy running
13   Rest day
14   6 miles easy running
15   6 miles easy running
16   6 × 440 in :90; 440 jog R
17   Rest day
18   4 miles easy running incorporating 2 miles in 14:00
19   3 miles easy running
20   Rest day
21   6 miles easy running incorporating 3 miles in 21:00

### SPECIALIZED TRAINING

You are now ready to proceed with the six weeks of specialized training leading to the 6-minute mile. If you have encountered injury, extra stress, or illness during your pre-conditioning phases, you may want to repeat the final two weeks of the above schedule before embarking on the specialized training.

## 1st Week

*Day*

1    6 miles easy running
2    880 in 3:10; 440 in :85; 220 in :40; all 660 R
3    3 miles easy running
4    6 × 110 in :18.5; 220 R; 5:00 rest; 6 × 110 in :18.5; 220 R
5    3 miles easy running
6    4 miles easy running incorporating 2 × 1 mile in 6:40
7    4 miles easy running

## 2nd Week

*Day*

1    5 miles in 37:30
2    660 in 2:25; 110 R; 110 in :19.5; 550 R — repeat set 2 more times
3    3 miles easy running
4    3 miles easy running
5    4 × 220 in :42; 440 R; 5:00 rest; 880 time trial
6    Rest day
7    6 miles in 45:00

## 3rd Week

### Day

1   4 miles easy running incorporating 2 miles in 13:45
2   10 × 220 in :40; 220 R
3   3 miles easy running
4   ¾ mile in 4:50; 660 R; 880 in 3:06
5   5 miles easy running
6   440 in :90; 110 R; 110 in :19.5; 440 R — repeat set 5 more times
7   Rest day

## 4th Week

### Day

1   8 miles in 64:00
2   3 × 880 in 3:06; 880 R
3   4 miles easy running
4   1½ miles in 10:20
5   4 miles easy running
6   Rest day
7   2 × ¾ mile in 4:50; 880 R

## 5th Week

### Day

1   4 miles easy running incorporating 2 miles in 13:45
2   8 × 440 in :92; 440 R
3   3 miles easy running
4   3 miles easy running
5   ¾ mile in 4:30; 10:00 rest; 880 in 3:00
6   4 miles easy running
7   5 miles in 35:00

## 6th Week

### Day

1   5 miles easy running
2   4 × 440 in :82; 440 walk R
3   3 miles easy running
4   10 × 110 in :20.5; 110 R
5   Rest day
6   2 miles easy running
7   Mile race in 6:00

*Cheryl Hansen, registered nurse. (Photograph by Bruce Glikin)*

# The 6:30 Mile or 5:59 1,500 Meters

*You are ready to train for a 6:30 mile if you can run:*

*220 yards in 40 seconds*
*440 yards in 86 seconds*

*To run a 6:30 mile, you will need to average 97.5 seconds per quarter*

In this series of schedules, the 6:30 mile is the slowest time. While there may be persuasive arguments for including schedules for slower mile times, it is a track-running fact of life that if you don't possess the basic speed (220 yards in 40 seconds, 440 yards in 86) to begin training for the 6:30 mile, the mile is not likely to be your event.

If this is the fastest mile standard you can qualify for, however, there is some heartening news: Experience has repeatedly shown us that if you wish to improve your miling time and if you can run the pre-training standards with a minimum of discomfort, you can improve rapidly after beginning the 6:30 schedule. It is not unusual for a runner with no track experience to find, after completing four to six weeks of the 6:30 schedule, that he or she is capable of progressing to the next-fastest schedule — the 6-minute mile — achieving the pre-conditioning workouts there, and thus raising his or her goals before having run a mile in competition.

## PRE-CONDITIONING

During the six weeks that prepare a runner for specialized training, the weekly mileage should range from 20 to 30 miles. Each track workout should begin with a 1- to 2-mile easy warm-up and end with a 1- to 2-mile easy warm-down. "Easy running" in this schedule is 8:15 to 9:00 per mile. "R" means jog recovery unless otherwise specified; when "R" represents a time, the interval should be spent walking or resting.

*Phase 1.* The first twenty-one days:

*Day*

1   3 miles easy running
2   10 × 110 in :23; 110 walk R
3   3 × 440 in :95; 220 walk R
4   3 miles easy running
5   2 miles in 15:30
6   6 × 110 in :23; 110 walk R
7   Rest day
8   4 miles easy running
9   10 × 110 in :23; 110 walk R
10   3 miles easy running
11   3 × 660 in 2:40; 440 walk R

12   Rest day
13   3 miles in 24:00
14   4 miles easy running
15   8 × 220 in :45; 220 walk R
16   4 miles easy running incorporating 2 miles in 15:30
17   3 miles easy running
18   6 × 440 in :95; 220 walk R
19   3 miles easy running
20   Rest day
21   5 miles in 40:00

*Phase 2*

*Day*

1   5 miles easy running
2   10 × 110 in :21; 110 jog R
3   3 miles easy running
4   4 × 660 in 2:40; 440 jog R
5   3 miles easy running
6   Rest day
7   6 miles easy running
8   4 miles in 32:00
9   440 in :95; 110 jog R; 110 in :21; 440 jog R — repeat set 5 more times
10   3 miles easy running
11   10 × 110 in :21; 110 R

12   3 miles easy running
13   Rest day
14   5 miles easy running
15   5 miles easy running
16   6 × 440 in :96; 440 R
17   Rest day
18   4 miles easy running incorporating 2 miles in 15:00
19   3 miles easy running
20   Rest day
21   5 miles easy running incorporating 3 miles in 24:00

SPECIALIZED TRAINING

The schedule for the 6:30 mile is a six-week program.

*1st Week*

*Day*

1   5 miles easy running
2   880 in 3:30; 440 in :90; 220 in :43; all 660 R
3   3 miles easy running
4   6 × 110 in :21; 220 R; 5:00 rest; 6 × 110 in :21; 220 R
5   3 miles easy running
6   3 miles easy running incorporating 1 mile in 7:00
7   4 miles easy running

## 2nd Week

*Day*

1   4 miles in 38:00
2   660 in 2:40; 110 R; 110 in :21.5;
    550 R — repeat set 2 more times
3   3 miles easy running
4   3 miles easy running
5   4 × 220 in :45; 440 R; 5:00 rest;
    880 time trial
6   Rest day
7   5 miles in 41:15

## 3rd Week

1   3 miles easy running incorporat-
    ing 1 mile in 7:00
2   8 × 220 in :45; 220 R
3   3 miles easy running
4   ¾ mile in 5:15; 660 R; 880 in
    3:20
5   4 miles easy running
6   440 in :96; 110 R; 110 in :21.5;
    440 R — repeat set 5 more times
7   Rest day

## 4th Week

*Day*

1   7 miles in 57:45
2   3 × 880 in 3:25; 880 R

3   3 miles easy running
4   1½ miles in 11:15
5   3 miles easy running
6   Rest day
7   2 × ¾ mile in 5:05; 880 R

## 5th Week

*Day*

1   3 miles easy running incorporat-
    ing 1 mile in 7:00
2   6 × 440 in :96; 440 R
3   3 miles easy running
4   3 miles easy running
5   ¾ mile in 4:50; 10:00 rest; 880
    in 3:15
6   3 miles easy running
7   4 miles in 30:00

## 6th Week

*Day*

1   4 miles easy running
2   4 × 440 in :85; 440 walk R
3   3 miles easy running
4   8 × 110 in :22; 110 jog R
5   Rest day
6   2 miles easy running
7   Mile race in 6:30

*Said Aouita (549), world-record holder at 1,500 meters and 5,000 meters, has the speed that racers need to win longer track races. (Photograph by George Herringshaw; courtesy* Track and Field News)

# SIX

# *3,000 Meters — 2 Miles —*
# *3 Miles — 5,000 Meters*

THE TRAINING SCHEDULES FOR LONGER-DISTANCE track events set out in this chapter have a rich history of coaching and competition.

Modern-day track runners can thank the competitive pioneers who introduced a new dimension to training and competition between 1920 and the middle of the 1960s. Their contributions have made the sport an easier road for runners of the last decade and of the future.

Paavo Nurmi, the legendary runner of the twenties, was the first to make a significant breakthrough in the longer track runs. His great contribution was making runners aware of the importance of *discipline* — a trait he showed in his training, his competition, and in his all-important emphasis on pace judgment in races as short as 1,500 meters. The next contribution came in the forties from Gundar Haaeg, the first to run under 14 minutes in the 5,000 meters, who proved that *speed* was an important part of the necessary makeup of a good long-distance track runner (Haaeg was a world-record holder in the mile). In the sixties Ron Clarke contributed the third factor: Training for the whole body, using speed and endurance running workouts combined with weight training for general musculoskeletal strength. Clarke's training regimen not only gave him great speed — he was the first under 13 minutes for 3 miles and the first to break 13:20 for 5,000 meters — but great racing range as well; he held world records at distances ranging from 2 miles to 20 kilometers (12.4 miles).

Other innovators like Arthur Lydiard, Percy Wells Cerutty, and Mihaly Igloi have made significant contributions to racing the longer track distances, but perhaps the greatest single contribution to running at this distance is that made by the use of the interval-training philosophy of Emil Zatopek, even though this great runner of the fifties never set a world record at distances of 5,000 meters or less.

Each of the schedules in the following pages is preceded by a set of time standards that will tell you whether you are ready to begin training for that specific goal. High school runners, however, should treat these standards as more accurate for the 2-mile distance and perhaps not as feasible for the 3-mile and 5,000-meter distances. Remember that you are just beginning to develop your physiological potential, and age is a crucial factor. As you mature, you will find that your work now has laid a base for future success.

*Allan Lawrence, fitness consultant, at the 1956 Australian Olympic Trials. (Photograph courtesy* The Age, *Melbourne, Australia)*

# The 14:00 5K
# The 13:31 3 Miles
# The 8:48 2 Miles

*You are ready to train for the above if you can run:*

*440 yards in 55 seconds*
*1 mile in 4:12*

*To run 5K in 14:00 and 3 miles in 13:31, you will need to average approximately 67.5 seconds per quarter*
*To run 2 miles in 8:48, you will need to average 66 seconds per quarter*

An eight-week base of 55 to 70 miles weekly should be undertaken before you begin the eight-week schedule leading to the above time goals. A typical week during this conditioning period should consist of:

- 1 long stamina run of 9–13 miles at 6:15–6:45 per mile
- 2 endurance workouts on the track (select *one* of the following per workout):
  - 15 × 220 in :32–:33; 440 R
  - 20 × 440 in :75; 220 R
  - 8 × 880 in 2:25; 440 R
  - 5 × 1 mile in 5:10; 660 R
  - 440 in :70; 880 in 2:30; ¾ mile in 3:55; 1 mile in 5:20; all 440 R; jog 880; 1 mile in 5:00; ¾ mile in 3:36; 880 in 2:15; 440 in :65; all 440 R
- 1 medium-distance run (6–9 miles) at 5:30–5:45 per mile
- 3 days of medium-distance (6–9 miles) maintenance runs at 6:15–6:45 per mile

In addition to this training, you should run 3 to 5 miles two mornings per week (on any of the off-track days) and incorporate 6 to 10 fast and controlled strides of 70 to 110 yards.

You are now ready to proceed with the final eight weeks of specialized training leading to the 5K, 3-mile, and 2-mile time goals.

In both the conditioning and specialized schedules, each track workout should begin with a 1- to 2-mile easy warm-up and end with

a 1- to 2-mile easy warm-down. Also in both schedules, "R" means jog recovery unless otherwise specified; when "R" represents a time, the interval should be spent walking or resting.

"Easy running" in this schedule is 6:15 to 7:15 per mile.

## 1st Week

### Day

1  14 miles easy running
2  A.M. 4 miles easy running incorporating 8 × 80 (fast and controlled)
   P.M. 6 miles in 33:00
3  12 × 220 in :28; 440 R
4  A.M. 4 miles easy running incorporating 5 × 100 (fast and controlled)
   P.M. 4 miles easy running
5  6 × 880 in 2:15; 880 R
6  6 miles easy running
7  10 miles in 57:30

## 2nd Week

### Day

1  8 miles easy running incorporating 10 × 110 (fast and controlled)
2  A.M. 3 miles easy running
   P.M. 660 in 1:45; 110 R; 220 in :30; 550 R — repeat set 5 more times
3  8 miles in 48:00
4  A.M. 3 miles easy running incorporating 6 × 100 (fast and controlled)
   P.M. 3 × 1 mile in 4:45; 880 R
5  A.M. 3 miles easy running incorporating 6 × 60 (fast and controlled)
   P.M. 7 miles easy running
6  7 miles easy running incorporating 3 miles in 15:00
7  8 miles in 48:00

## 3rd Week

### Day

1  16 × 330 in :45; 330 R
2  A.M. 3 miles easy running incorporating 6 × 100 (fast and controlled)
   P.M. 6 miles in 34:00
3  3 × 1¼ miles in 6:15; 660 R
4  A.M. 3 miles easy running incorporating 8 × 100 (fast and controlled)
   P.M. 7 miles easy running
5  8 × 440 in :62; 440 R
6  5 miles easy running
7  2-mile time trial *or* competitive effort at 1–2 miles

## 4th Week

### Day

1  10 miles easy running
2  A.M. 4 miles easy running incorporating 8 × 100 (fast and controlled)
   P.M. 6 miles in 35:00
3  6 × 880 in 2:15; 660 R
4  A.M. 3 miles easy running incorporating 6 × 150 (fast and controlled)
   P.M. 8 miles easy running
5  A.M. 3 miles easy running incorporating 6 × 100 (fast and controlled)
   P.M. 4 × 1 mile in 4:45; 440 R
6  10 miles easy running
7  8 miles easy running incorporating 3 miles in 14:45

## 5th Week

### Day

1   12 miles easy running
2   16 × 440 in :66; 440 R
3   A.M. 3 miles easy running incorporating 6 × 100 (fast and controlled)
    P.M. 7 miles easy running
4   2 × 1½ miles in 7:00; 880 R
5   8 miles easy running incorporating 6 × 100 (fast and controlled)
6   2 × 1 mile in 4:30; 1 mile R
7   6 miles easy running

## 6th Week

### Day

1   10 miles in 55:00
2   A.M. 3 miles easy running with 8 × 70 (fast and controlled)
    P.M. 6 × 550 in :80; 660 R
3   6 miles easy running
4   2 × 1½ miles in 7:00; 880 R
5   A.M. 3 miles easy running incorporating 6 × 100 (fast and controlled)
    P.M. 7 miles easy running
6   Rest day
7   Competitive effort (at 1–3 miles) *or* 2 miles in 9:00

## 7th Week

### Day

1   10 miles easy running
2   A.M. 4 miles easy running incorporating 6 × 110 (fast and controlled)
    P.M. 6 miles easy running
3   A.M. 3 miles easy running incorporating 6 × 100 (fast and controlled)
    P.M. 3 × 1 mile in 4:35; 440 R
4   8 miles easy running incorporating 4 miles in 22:00
5   6 miles easy running
6   A.M. 3 miles easy running incorporating 5 × 100 (fast and controlled)
    P.M. 6 miles easy running
7   8 × 440 in :60; 440 R

## 8th Week

### Day

1   10 miles in 60:00
2   A.M. 3 miles easy running with 6 × 100 (fast and controlled)
    P.M. 5 × 880 in 2:08; 440 R
3   5 miles easy running
4   A.M. 3 miles easy running incorporating 5 × 100 (fast and controlled)
    P.M. 3 miles easy running
5   Rest day
6   4 miles easy running
7   5K race in 14:00

*Robert Briggs, carpenter. (Photograph by Tracey Wong Briggs)*

# The 14:30 5K
# The 14:00 3 Miles
# The 9:04 2 Miles

*You are ready to train for the above if you can run:*

*440 yards in 57 seconds*
*1 mile in 4:20*

*To run 5K in 14:30 and 3 miles in 14:00, you will need to average approximately 70 seconds per quarter*
*To run 2 miles in 9:04, you will need to average 68 seconds per quarter*

An eight-week base of 55 to 70 miles is recommended before you begin the eight-week schedule to accomplish the above time goals. A typical seven-day sample during this conditioning phase consists of:

- 1 long stamina run of 9–13 miles at 6:30–7:00 per mile
- 2 endurance workouts on the track (select *one* of the following per track workout):
  - 15 × 220 in :34; 440 R
  - 20 × 440 in :78; 220 R
  - 8 × 880 in 2:32; 440 R
  - 5 × 1 mile in 5:20; 660 R
  - 440 in :75; 880 in 2:35; ¾ mile in 4:05; 1 mile in 5:25; all 440 R; jog 880; 1 mile in 5:10; ¾ mile in 3:45; 880 in 2:20; 440 in :68; all 440 R
- 1 medium-distance run (6–9 miles) at 5:45–6:00 per mile
- 3 days of medium-distance (6–9 miles) maintenance runs at 6:30–7:00 per mile

In addition to the above conditioning training, you should do two morning runs (on nontrack days) of 3 to 5 miles each, incorporating 6 to 10 fast and controlled strides of 70 to 100 yards.

After the eight-week conditioning period, you are ready to begin the final eight weeks of specialized training.

In both the conditioning and specialized schedules, each track workout should begin with a 1- to 2-mile easy warm-up and end with a 1- to 2-mile easy warm-down. Also in both schedules, "R" means jog recovery unless otherwise specified; when "R" represents a time, the interval should be spent walking or resting.

"Easy running" in this schedule is 6:30 to 7:30 per mile.

## 1st Week

### Day

1  12 miles easy running
2  A.M. 3 miles easy running incorporating 6 × 100 (fast and controlled)
   P.M. 6 miles in 34:00
3  12 × 220 in :30; 440 R
4  A.M. 4 miles easy running incorporating 6 × 100 (fast and controlled)
   P.M. 4 miles easy running
5  6 × 880 in 2:22; 880 R
6  6 miles easy running
7  10 miles in 60:00

## 2nd Week

### Day

1  8 miles easy running incorporating 6 × 100 (fast and controlled)
2  A.M. 3 miles easy running
   P.M. 660 in 1:45; 110 R; 220 in :32; 550 R — repeat set 5 more times
3  8 miles in 49:00
4  A.M. 3 miles easy running incorporating 6 × 100 (fast and controlled)
   P.M. 7 miles easy running
5  A.M. 3 miles easy running incorporating 6 × 80 (fast and controlled)
   P.M. 6 miles easy running
6  6 miles easy running incorporating 3 miles in 15:30
7  8 miles in 50:00

## 3rd Week

### Day

1  16 × 330 in :47.5; 330 R
2  6 miles in 35:00
3  3 × 1¼ miles in 6:30; 660 R
4  A.M. 3 miles easy running incorporating 8 × 100 (fast and controlled)
   P.M. 6 miles easy running
5  8 × 440 in :63; 440 R
6  5 miles easy running
7  2-mile time trial *or* competitive effort at 1 to 2 miles

## 4th Week

### Day

1  10 miles easy running
2  A.M. 3 miles easy running incorporating 8 × 100 (fast and controlled)
   P.M. 6 miles in 36:00
3  6 miles easy running
4  A.M. 3 miles easy running incorporating 6 × 150 (fast and controlled)
   P.M. 7 miles easy running
5  A.M. 3 miles easy running incorporating 6 × 100 (fast and controlled)
   P.M. 4 × 1 mile in 5:00; 440 R
6  10 miles easy running
7  8 miles easy running incorporating 3 miles in 15:15

## 5th Week

*Day*

1  10 miles easy running
2  16 × 440 in :68; 440 R
3  A.M. 3 miles easy running incorporating 6 × 100 (fast and controlled)
    P.M. 6 miles easy running
4  2 × 1½ miles in 7:15; 880 R
5  8 miles easy running incorporating 6 × 100 (fast and controlled)
6  2 × 1 mile in 4:38; 1 mile R
7  6 miles easy running

## 6th Week

*Day*

1  10 miles in 57:30
2  A.M. 3 miles easy running with 6 × 100 (fast and controlled)
    P.M. 6 × 550 in :85; 660 R
3  6 miles easy running
4  2 × 1½ miles in 7:15; 880 R
5  A.M. 3 miles easy running incorporating 6 × 100 (fast and controlled)
    P.M. 7 miles easy running
6  Rest day
7  Competitive effort at 1–3 miles *or* 2 miles in 9:30

## 7th Week

*Day*

1  10 miles easy running
2  A.M. 4 miles easy running incorporating 6 × 100 (fast and controlled)
    P.M. 3 × 1 mile in 4:50; 440 R
3  6 miles easy running
4  A.M. 3 miles easy running incorporating 10 × 100 (fast and controlled)
    P.M. 7 miles easy running
5  6 miles easy running
6  7 miles easy running incorporating 4 miles in 23:00
7  8 × 440 in :63; 440 R

## 8th Week

*Day*

1  10 miles in 62:30
2  A.M. 3 miles easy running incorporating 6 × 100 (fast and controlled)
    P.M. 5 × 880 in 2:15; 440 R
3  5 miles easy running
4  A.M. 3 miles easy running incorporating 5 × 100 (fast and controlled)
    P.M. 3 miles easy running
5  Rest day
6  4 miles easy running
7  5K race in 14:30

*Keith Broussard, house painter. (Photograph by Brent Roy, Point Coupee Banner, New Roads, Louisiana)*

# The 15:00 5K
# The 14:29 3 Miles
# The 9:20 2 Miles

*You are ready to train for the above distances if you can run:*

*440 yards in 60 seconds*
*1 mile in 4:30*

*To run 5K in 15:00 and 3 miles in 14:29 you will need to average approximately 72.5 seconds per quarter*
*To run 9:20 for 2 miles, you will need to average 70 seconds per quarter*

You should have an eight-week base of 55 to 70 miles weekly before you begin the eight weeks of specialized training leading to the above time goals. A typical week during this period should contain:

- 1 long stamina run of 9–13 miles at 6:45–7:15 per mile
- 2 endurance workouts on the track (select *one* of the following per track workout):
  - 15 × 220 in :35; 440 R
  - 20 × 440 in :80–:82; 220 R
  - 8 × 880 in 2:40; 440 R
  - 5 × 1 mile in 5:30; 660 R
  - 440 in :78; 880 in 2:44; ¾ mile in 4:15; 1 mile in 5:50; all 440 R; jog 880; 1 mile in 5:20; ¾ mile in 3:52; 880 in 2:30; 440 in :70; all 440 R
- 1 medium-distance run (6–9 miles) at 6:00–6:15 per mile
- 3 days of medium-distance (6–9 miles) maintenance runs at 6:45–7:15 per mile

Again we recommend that two early morning runs of 3 to 5 miles with 6 to 8 fast strides of 70 to 100 yards be incorporated in this conditioning.

You are now ready to undertake the final eight weeks of specialized training.

In both the conditioning and specialized schedules, each track workout should begin with a 1- to 2-mile easy warm-up and end with a 1- to 2-mile easy warm-down. Also in both schedules, "R" means jog recovery unless otherwise specified; when "R" represents a time, the interval should be spent walking or resting.

"Easy running" in this schedule is 6:45 to 7:45 per mile.

## 1st Week
### Day

1  10 miles easy running
2  A.M. 3 miles easy running incorporating 6 × 100 (fast and controlled)
   P.M. 6 miles in 36:00
3  12 × 220 in :32; 440 R
4  A.M. 3 miles easy running incorporating 5 × 100 (fast and controlled)
   P.M. 4 miles easy running
5  6 × 880 in 2:30; 880 R
6  6 miles easy running
7  10 miles in 62:30

## 2nd Week
### Day

1  8 miles easy running incorporating 10 × 100 (fast and controlled)
2  A.M. 3 miles easy running
   P.M. 660 in 1:48; 110 R; 220 in :33; 550 R — repeat set 5 more times
3  8 miles in 50:00
4  A.M. 3 miles easy running incorporating 5 × 100 (fast and controlled)
   P.M. 6 miles easy running
5  A.M. 3 miles easy running incorporating 6 × 80 (fast and controlled)
   P.M. 6 miles easy running
6  6 miles easy running incorporating 3 miles in 16:00
7  8 miles in 52:00

## 3rd Week
### Day

1  16 × 330 in :50; 330 R
2  6 miles in 36:00
3  3 × 1¼ miles in 6:35; 660 R
4  A.M. 3 miles easy running incorporating 6 × 100 (fast and controlled)
   P.M. 6 miles easy running
5  8 × 440 in :66; 440 R
6  5 miles easy running
7  2-mile time trial *or* competitive effort at 1–2 miles

## 4th Week
### Day

1  10 miles easy running
2  A.M. 3 miles easy running incorporating 8 × 100 (fast and controlled)
   P.M. 6 miles in 37:00
3  7 miles easy running
4  A.M. 3 miles easy running incorporating 4 × 150 (fast and controlled)
   P.M. 6 miles easy running
5  4 × 1 mile in 5:08; 440 R
6  9 miles easy running
7  8 miles easy running incorporating 3 miles in 15:45

## 5th Week
### Day

1  9 miles easy running
2  16 × 440 in :70; 440 R

3   A.M. 3 miles easy running incorporating 6 × 100 (fast and controlled)
    P.M. 6 miles easy running
4   2 × 1½ miles in 7:30; 880 R
5   8 miles easy running incorporating 6 × 100 (fast and controlled)
6   2 × 1 mile in 4:45; 1 mile R
7   6 miles easy running

## 6th Week

*Day*

1   10 miles in 60:00
2   A.M. 3 miles easy running incorporating 6 × 100 (fast and controlled)
    P.M. 6 × 550 in :88; 660 R
3   6 miles easy running
4   2 × 1½ miles in 7:30; 880 R
5   A.M. 3 miles easy running incorporating 6 × 100 (fast and controlled)
    P.M. 7 miles easy running
6   Rest day
7   Competitive effort at 1–3 miles *or* 2 miles in 9:45

## 7th Week

*Day*

1   10 miles easy running
2   A.M. 4 miles easy running incorporating 6 × 100 (fast and controlled)
    P.M. 3 × 1 mile in 5:00; 440 R

3   6 miles easy running
4   A.M. 3 miles easy running incorporating 10 × 100 (fast and controlled)
    P.M. 7 miles easy running
5   6 miles easy running
6   7 miles easy running incorporating 4 miles in 23:30
7   8 × 440 in :65; 440 R

## 8th Week

*Day*

1   10 miles in 64:00
2   A.M. 3 miles easy running incorporating 6 × 100 (fast and controlled)
    P.M. 5 × 880 in 2:20; 440 R
3   5 miles easy running
4   A.M. 3 miles easy running incorporating 5 × 100 (fast and controlled)
    P.M. 3 miles easy running
5   Rest day
6   4 miles easy running
7   5K race in 15:00

*John Nodecker, special education teacher. (Photograph by Joanne Kelly-Nodecker)*

# The 15:30 5K
# The 14:58 3 Miles
# The 9:40 2 Miles

*You are ready to train for the above distances if you can run:*

*440 yards in 62 seconds*
*1 mile in 4:40*

*To run 5K in 15:30 and 3 miles in 14:58, you will need to average approximately 75 seconds per quarter*
*To run 2 miles in 9:40, you will need to average 72.5 seconds per quarter*

An eight-week base of 55 to 70 miles weekly should be completed before you begin the eight weeks of specialized training leading to the above time goals. A typical week during this period should contain the following training workouts:

- 1 long stamina run of 9–13 miles at 7:00–7:30 per mile
- 2 endurance workouts on the track (select *one* of the following per workout):
  - 15 × 220 in :36; 440 R
  - 20 × 440 in :85; 220 R
  - 5 × 1 mile in 5:40; 660 R
  - 8 × 880 in 2:45; 440 R
  - 440 in :82; 880 in 2:50; ¾ mile in 4:30; 1 mile in 6:10; all 440 R; jog 880; 1 mile in 5:30; ¾ mile in 4:00; 880 in 2:35; 440 in :72; all 440 R
- 1 medium-distance run (6–9 miles) at 6:15–6:30 per mile
- 3 days of medium-distance (6–9 miles) maintenance runs at 7:00–7:30 per mile

Two morning runs of 3 to 5 miles with 6 to 8 strides of 70 to 100 yards incorporated in these runs are recommended. The morning runs should be scheduled on nontrack days.

After the eight-week conditioning period, you can begin the final eight weeks of specialized training.

In both the conditioning and specialized schedules, each track workout should begin with a 1- to 2-mile easy warm-up and end with

a 1- to 2-mile easy warm-down. Also in both schedules, "R" means jog recovery unless otherwise specified; when "R" represents a time, the interval should be spent walking or resting.

"Easy running" in this schedule is 7:00 to 7:45 per mile.

## 1st Week

### Day

1   10 miles easy running
2   A.M. 3 miles easy running incorporating 6 × 100 (fast and controlled)
    P.M. 6 miles in 37:00
3   12 × 220 in :33; 440 R
4   A.M. 3 miles easy running incorporating 5 × 100 (fast and controlled)
    P.M. 4 miles easy running
5   6 × 880 in 2:35; 880 R
6   6 miles easy running
7   10 miles in 64:00

## 2nd Week

### Day

1   8 miles easy running incorporating 8 × 100 (fast and controlled)
2   A.M. 3 miles easy running
    P.M. 660 in 1:52; 110 R; 220 in :34; 550 R — repeat set 5 more times
3   8 miles in 53:00
4   A.M. 3 miles easy running incorporating 5 × 100 (fast and controlled)
    P.M. 6 miles easy running
5   A.M. 3 miles easy running incorporating 6 × 80 (fast and controlled)
    P.M. 6 miles easy running
6   6 miles easy running incorporating 3 miles in 16:30
7   8 miles in 53:00

## 3rd Week

### Day

1   16 × 330 in :52; 330 R
2   6 miles in 36:45
3   3 × 1¼ miles in 6:45; 660 R
4   A.M. 3 miles easy running incorporating 6 × 100 (fast and controlled)
    P.M. 6 miles easy running
5   8 × 440 in :67; 440 R
6   5 miles easy running
7   2-mile time trial *or* competitive effort at 1–2 miles

## 4th Week

### Day

1   10 miles easy running
2   A.M. 3 miles easy running incorporating 8 × 100 (fast and controlled)
    P.M. 6 miles in 37:30
3   7 miles easy running
4   A.M. 3 miles easy running incorporating 8 × 100 (fast and controlled)
    P.M. 6 miles easy running
5   4 × 1 mile in 5:14; 440 R
6   9 miles easy running
7   8 miles easy running incorporating 3 miles in 16:00

## 5th Week

### Day

1   9 miles easy running
2   16 × 440 in :72; 440 R
3   A.M. 3 miles easy running incorporating 6 × 100 (fast and controlled)
    P.M. 6 miles easy running

4   2 × 1½ miles in 7:45; 880 R

5   8 miles easy running incorporating 6 × 100 (fast and controlled)

6   2 × 1 mile in 4:50; 1 mile R

7   6 miles easy running

## 6th Week

*Day*

1   10 miles in 62:00

2   A.M. 3 miles easy running incorporating 6 × 100 (fast and controlled)
P.M. 6 × 550 in :90; 660 R

3   6 miles easy running

4   2 × 1½ miles in 7:45; 880 R

5   A.M. 3 miles easy running incorporating 6 × 100 (fast and controlled)
P.M. 7 miles easy running

6   Rest day

7   Competitive effort at 1–3 miles *or* 2 miles in 10:00

## 7th Week

*Day*

1   10 miles easy running

2   A.M. 4 miles easy running incorporating 6 × 100 (fast and controlled)

P.M. 3 × 1 mile in 5:10; 440 R

3   6 miles easy running

4   A.M. 3 miles easy running incorporating 10 × 100 (fast and controlled)
P.M. 7 miles easy running

5   6 miles easy running

6   7 miles easy running incorporating 4 miles in 23:50

7   8 × 440 in :66; 440 R

## 8th Week

*Day*

1   10 miles in 65:00

2   A.M. 3 miles easy running incorporating 6 × 100 (fast and controlled)
P.M. 5 × 880 in 2:25; 440 R

3   5 miles easy running

4   A.M. 3 miles easy running incorporating 5 × 100 (fast and controlled)
P.M. 3 miles easy running

5   Rest day

6   4 miles easy running

7   5K race in 15:30

*Carol Urish-McLatchie, geologist. (Photograph by Conrad J. McCarthy)*

# The 16:00 5K
# The 15:27 3 Miles
# The 10:00 2 Miles

---

*You are ready to train for the above distances if you can run:*

*440 yards in 64.5 seconds*
*1 mile in 4:52*

*To run 5K in 16:00 and 3 miles in 15:27, you will need to average approximately 77.5 seconds per quarter*
*To run 2 miles in 10:00, you will need to average 75 seconds per quarter*

---

As in the preceding 5K schedules, the conditioning period recommended for the above time goals is eight weeks with weekly mileage in the 50-to-65 range. A typical week's training during this period should contain:

- 1 long stamina run of 9–13 miles at 7:00–7:45 per mile
- 2 endurance workouts on the track (select *one* of the following per workout):
  - 15 × 220 in :37; 440 R
  - 20 × 440 in :86; 220 R
  - 8 × 880 in 2:50; 440 R
  - 5 × 1 mile in 5:45; 660 R
  - 440 in :83; 880 in 2:52; ¾ mile in 4:30; 1 mile in 6:10; all 440 R; jog 880; 1 mile in 5:35; ¾ mile in 4:05; 880 in 2:38; 440 in :73; all 440 R
- 1 medium-distance run (6–9 miles) at 6:30–6:45 per mile
- 3 days of medium-distance (6–9 miles) maintenance runs at 7:00–7:45 per mile

Twice per week a morning run of 3 to 5 miles incorporating 6 to 8 strides between 70 and 100 yards is recommended. The morning runs should be on nontrack days.

Once the conditioning period has been completed, the final eight weeks of specialized training may begin.

In both the conditioning and specialized schedules, each track workout should begin with a 1- to 2-mile easy warm-up and end with

a 1- to 2-mile easy warm-down. Also in both schedules, "R" means jog recovery unless otherwise specified; when "R" represents a time, the interval should be spent walking or resting.

"Easy running" in this schedule is 7:15 to 8:00 per mile.

## 1st Week
### Day

1   10 miles easy running
2   A.M. 3 miles easy running incorporating 6 × 100 (fast and controlled)
    P.M. 6 miles in 37:30
3   12 × 220 in :34; 440 R
4   A.M. 3 miles easy running incorporating 5 × 100 (fast and controlled)
    P.M. 4 miles easy running
5   6 × 880 in 2:40; 880 R
6   6 miles easy running
7   10 miles in 65:00

## 2nd Week
### Day

1   8 miles easy running incorporating 8 × 100 (fast and controlled)
2   A.M. 3 miles easy running
    P.M. 660 in 1:54; 110 R; 220 in :35; 550 R — repeat set 5 more times
3   8 miles in 51:30
4   A.M. 3 miles easy running incorporating 5 × 100 (fast and controlled)
    P.M. 6 miles easy running
5   A.M. 3 miles easy running incorporating 6 × 100 (fast and controlled)
    P.M. 6 miles easy running

6   6 miles easy running incorporating 3 miles in 16:45
7   8 miles in 54:00

## 3rd Week
### Day

1   16 × 330 in :53; 330 R
2   6 miles in 37:00
3   3 × 1¼ miles in 6:50; 660 R
4   A.M. 3 miles easy running incorporating 6 × 100 (fast and controlled)
    P.M. 6 miles easy running
5   8 × 440 in :69; 440 R
6   5 miles easy running
7   2-mile time trial *or* competitive effort at 1–2 miles

## 4th Week
### Day

1   10 miles easy running
2   A.M. 3 miles easy running incorporating 8 × 100 (fast and controlled)
    P.M. 6 miles in 38:00
3   7 miles easy running
4   A.M. 3 miles easy running incorporating 8 × 100 (fast and controlled)
    P.M. 6 miles easy running
5   4 × 1 mile in 5:20; 440 R
6   9 miles easy running
7   8 miles easy running incorporating 3 miles in 16:15

## 5th Week

*Day*

1  9 miles easy running
2  16 × 440 in :74; 440 R
3  A.M. 3 miles easy running incorporating 6 × 100 (fast and controlled)
P.M. 6 miles easy running
4  2 × 1½ miles in 7:55; 880 R
5  8 miles easy running incorporating 6 × 100 (fast and controlled)
6  2 × 1 mile in 5:00; 1 mile R
7  6 miles easy running

## 6th Week

*Day*

1  10 miles in 63:00
2  A.M. 3 miles easy running incorporating 6 × 100 (fast and controlled)
P.M. 6 × 550 in :92; 660 R
3  6 miles easy running
4  2 × 1½ miles in 7:55; 880 R
5  A.M. 3 miles easy running incorporating 6 × 100 (fast and controlled)
P.M. 7 miles easy running
6  Rest day
7  Competitive effort at 1–3 miles *or* 2 miles in 10:15

## 7th Week

*Day*

1  10 miles easy running
2  A.M. 4 miles easy running incorporating 6 × 100 (fast and controlled)
P.M. 3 × 1 mile in 5:15; 440 R
3  6 miles easy running
4  A.M. 3 miles easy running incorporating 10 × 100 (fast and controlled)
P.M. 7 miles easy running
5  6 miles easy running
6  7 miles easy running incorporating 4 miles in 24:00
7  8 × 440 in :69; 440 R

## 8th Week

*Day*

1  10 miles in 66:00
2  A.M. 3 miles easy running incorporating 6 × 100 (fast and controlled)
P.M. 5 × 880 in 2:30; 440 R
3  5 miles easy running
4  A.M. 3 miles easy running incorporating 5 × 100 (fast and controlled)
P.M. 3 miles easy running
5  Rest day
6  4 miles easy running
7  5K race in 16:00

*Joel Gremillion, high school student. (Photograph by Tim Gremillion)*

# The 17:00 5K
# The 16:25 3 Miles
# The 10:32 2 Miles

*You are ready to train for the above distances if you can run:*

*440 yards in 66.5 seconds*
*1 mile in 5:05*

*To run 5K in 17:00 and 3 miles in 16:25, you will need to average approximately 82 seconds per quarter*
*To run 2 miles in 10:32, you will need to average 79 seconds per quarter*

The recommended conditioning period before specialized training is eight weeks with a weekly range of 50 to 60 miles. A sample week's training during the conditioning period is:

- 1 long stamina run of 9–13 miles at 7:15–7:45 per mile
- 2 endurance workouts on the track (select *one* of the following per track workout):
    - 15 × 220 in :38; 440 R
    - 20 × 440 in :90; 220 R
    - 6 × 880 in 2:55; 440 R
    - 4 × 1 mile in 5:50; 660 R
    - 440 in :86; 880 in 3:00; ¾ mile in 4:45; 1 mile in 6:20; all 440 R; jog 880; 1 mile in 5:45; ¾ mile in 4:10; 880 in 2:43; 440 in :75; all 440 R
- 1 medium-distance run (6–9 miles) at 6:30–7:15 per mile
- 3 days of medium-distance (6–9 miles) maintenance runs at 7:15–7:45 per mile

In addition, two morning runs of 3 to 5 miles with 5 to 8 strides of 70 to 100 yards are recommended. These workouts should be done on the off-track days.

In both the conditioning and specialized schedules, each track workout should begin with a 1- to 2-mile easy warm-up and end with a 1- to 2-mile easy warm-down. Also in both schedules, "R" means jog recovery unless otherwise specified; when "R" represents a time, the interval should be spent walking or resting.

"Easy running" in the eight-week specialized training schedule is 7:30 to 8:00 per mile.

## 1st Week
### Day
1   8 miles easy running
2   A.M. 3 miles easy running incorporating 6 × 100 (fast and controlled)
    P.M. 6 miles in 39:00
3   12 × 220 in :36; 440 R
4   A.M. 3 miles easy running incorporating 5 × 100 (fast and controlled)
    P.M. 4 miles easy running
5   6 × 880 in 2:45; 880 R
6   6 miles easy running
7   8 miles in 53:00

## 2nd Week
### Day
1   6 miles easy running incorporating 8 × 100 (fast and controlled)
2   A.M. 3 miles easy running
    P.M. 660 in 1:58; 110 R; 220 in :36; 550 R — repeat set 5 more times
3   8 miles in 53:00
4   A.M. 3 miles easy running incorporating 5 × 100 (fast and controlled)
    P.M. 4 miles easy running
5   A.M. 3 miles easy running incorporating 6 × 100 (fast and controlled)
    P.M. 4 miles easy running
6   6 miles easy running incorporating 3 miles in 17:15
7   6 miles in 39:00

## 3rd Week
### Day
1   12 × 330 in :56; 330 R
2   6 miles in 38:30
3   3 × 1¼ miles in 7:05; 660 R
4   A.M. 3 miles easy running incorporating 6 × 100 (fast and controlled)
    P.M. 4 miles easy running
5   8 × 440 in :72; 440 R
6   5 miles easy running
7   2-mile time trial *or* competitive effort at 1–2 miles

## 4th Week
### Day
1   10 miles easy running
2   A.M. 3 miles easy running incorporating 8 × 100 (fast and controlled)
    P.M. 6 miles in 39:00
3   6 miles easy running
4   A.M. 3 miles easy running incorporating 8 × 100 (fast and controlled)
    P.M. 6 miles easy running
5   4 × 1 mile in 5:35; 440 R
6   8 miles easy running
7   6 miles easy running incorporating 3 miles in 17:15

## 5th Week
### Day
1   7 miles easy running
2   16 × 440 in :80; 440 R
3   A.M. 3 miles easy running incorporating 6 × 100 (fast and controlled)
    P.M. 4 miles easy running

4   2 × 1½ miles in 8:15; 880 R
5   6 miles easy running incorporating 6 × 100 (fast and controlled)
6   2 × 1 mile in 5:15; 1 mile R
7   6 miles easy running

## 6th Week

### Day

1   10 miles in 65:00
2   A.M. 3 miles easy running incorporating 6 × 100 (fast and controlled)
    P.M. 6 × 550 in :96; 660 R
3   6 miles easy running
4   2 × 1½ miles in 8:15; 880 R
5   A.M. 3 miles easy running incorporating 6 × 100 (fast and controlled)
    P.M. 5 miles easy running
6   Rest day
7   Competitive effort at 1–3 miles *or* 2 miles in 11:00

## 7th Week

### Day

1   8 miles easy running
2   A.M. 3 miles easy running incorporating 5 × 100 (fast and controlled)
    P.M. 3 × 1 mile in 5:25; 440 R
3   6 miles easy running

4   A.M. 3 miles easy running incorporating 10 × 100 (fast and controlled)
    P.M. 5 miles easy running
5   6 miles easy running
6   6 miles easy running incorporating 4 miles in 24:30
7   8 × 440 in :72; 440 R

## 8th Week

### Day

1   10 miles in 67:30
2   A.M. 3 miles easy running incorporating 6 × 100 (fast and controlled)
    P.M. 5 × 880 in 2:38; 440 R
3   5 miles easy running
4   A.M. 3 miles easy running incorporating 5 × 100 (fast and controlled)
    P.M. 3 miles easy running
5   Rest day
6   3 miles easy running
7   5K race in 17:00

*Donna Weatherford, bank examiner. (Photograph by Bruce Glikin)*

# The 18:00 5K
# The 17:23 3 Miles
# The 11:12 2 Miles

*You are ready to train for the above distances if you can run:*

*440 yards in 68.5 seconds*
*1 mile in 5:18*

*To run 5K in 18:00 and 3 miles in 17:23, you will need to average approximately 87 seconds per quarter*
*To run 2 miles in 11:12, you will need to average 84 seconds per quarter*

You should cover 50 to 60 miles weekly during an eight-week conditioning period before beginning the eight-week specialized training phase. A typical week's training should contain the following:

- 1 long stamina run of 9–13 miles at 7:30–8:00 per mile
- 2 endurance workouts on the track (select *one* of the following per track workout):
  - 15 × 220 in :40; 440 R
  - 16 × 440 in :92; 220 R
  - 6 × 880 in 3:05; 440 R
  - 4 × 1 mile in 6:10; 660 R
  - 440 in :90; 880 in 3:08; ¾ mile in 4:50; 1 mile in 6:30; all 440 R; jog 880; 1 mile in 6:00; ¾ mile in 4:20; 880 in 2:45; 440 in :78; all 440 R
- 1 medium-distance run (6–9 miles) at 6:45–7:30 per mile
- 3 days of medium-distance (6–9 miles) maintenance runs at 7:30–8:00 per mile

Two morning runs of 3 to 5 miles with 5 to 8 strides of 70 to 100 yards should also be included in the conditioning schedule. Again, these workouts should be done on nontrack days.

In both the conditioning and specialized schedules, each track workout should begin with a 1- to 2-mile easy warm-up and end with a 1- to 2-mile easy warm-down. Also in both schedules, "R" means jog recovery unless otherwise specified; when "R" represents a time, the interval should be spent walking or resting.

"Easy running" in the eight-week specialized training schedule is 7:45 to 8:15 per mile.

## 1st Week

### Day

1  8 miles easy running
2  A.M. 3 miles easy running incorporating 6 × 100 (fast and controlled)
   P.M. 6 miles in 40:00
3  12 × 220 in :38; 440 R
4  A.M. 3 miles easy running incorporating 6 × 100 (fast and controlled)
   P.M. 3 miles easy running
5  6 × 880 in 2:50; 880 R
6  6 miles easy running
7  8 miles in 54:00

## 2nd Week

### Day

1  6 miles easy running incorporating 8 × 100 (fast and controlled)
2  A.M. 3 miles easy running
   P.M. 660 in 2:00; 110 R; 220 in :38; 550 R — repeat set 5 more times
3  8 miles in 54:00
4  A.M. 3 miles easy running incorporating 5 × 100 (fast and controlled)
   P.M. 4 miles easy running
5  A.M. 3 miles easy running incorporating 6 × 100 (fast and controlled)
   P.M. 4 miles easy running
6  6 miles easy running incorporating 3 miles in 18:00
7  6 miles in 40:00

## 3rd Week

### Day

1  12 × 330 in :58; 330 R
2  6 miles in 39:15
3  3 × 1¼ miles in 7:20; 660 R
4  A.M. 3 miles easy running incorporating 6 × 100 (fast and controlled)
   P.M. 4 miles easy running
5  8 × 440 in :74; 440 R
6  5 miles easy running
7  2-mile time trial *or* competitive effort at 1–2 miles

## 4th Week

### Day

1  10 miles easy running
2  A.M. 3 miles easy running incorporating 8 × 100 (fast and controlled)
   P.M. 6 miles in 40:00
3  6 miles easy running
4  A.M. 3 miles easy running incorporating 8 × 100 (fast and controlled)
   P.M. 6 miles easy running
5  4 × 1 mile in 5:55; 440 R
6  8 miles easy running
7  6 miles easy running incorporating 3 miles in 18:15

## 5th Week

### Day

1  7 miles easy running
2  16 × 440 in :85; 440 R
3  A.M. 3 miles easy running incorporating 6 × 100 (fast and controlled)
   P.M. 4 miles easy running

4   2 × 1½ miles in 8:45; 880 R
5   6 miles easy running incorporating 6 × 100 (fast and controlled)
6   2 × 1 mile in 5:30; 1 mile R
7   6 miles easy running

## 6th Week

### Day

1   10 miles in 67:30
2   A.M. 3 miles easy running incorporating 6 × 100 (fast and controlled)
    P.M. 6 × 550 in :98; 660 R
3   6 miles easy running
4   2 × 1½ miles in 8:45; 880 R
5   A.M. 3 miles easy running incorporating 6 × 100 (fast and controlled)
    P.M. 5 miles easy running
6   Rest day
7   Competitive effort at 1–3 miles *or* 2 miles in 11:35

## 7th Week

### Day

1   8 miles easy running
2   A.M. 3 miles easy running incorporating 5 × 100 (fast and controlled)
    P.M. 3 × 1 mile in 5:50; 440 R
3   6 miles easy running

4   A.M. 3 miles easy running incorporating 10 × 100 (fast and controlled)
    P.M. 5 miles easy running
5   6 miles easy running
6   6 miles easy running incorporating 4 miles in 25:00
7   8 × 440 in :74; 440 R

## 8th Week

### Day

1   10 miles in 70:00
2   A.M. 3 miles easy running incorporating 6 × 100 (fast and controlled)
    P.M. 5 × 880 in 2:48; 440 R
3   5 miles easy running
4   A.M. 3 miles easy running incorporating 5 × 100 (fast and controlled)
    P.M. 3 miles easy running
5   Rest day
6   3 miles easy running
7   5K race in 18:00

*Mary Cullen, homemaker. (Photograph by Bruce Glikin)*

# The 19:00 5K
# The 18:21 3 Miles
# The 11:44 2 Miles

*You are ready to train for the above distances if you can run:*

*440 yards in 71.5 seconds*
*1 mile in 5:30*

*To run 5K in 19:00 and 3 miles in 18:21, you will need to average approximately 92 seconds per quarter*
*To run 2 miles in 11:44, you will need to average 88 seconds per quarter*

The weekly mileage during the conditioning period for the above time goals is 45 to 50 miles. A typical week's training during this eight-week period should contain:

- 1 long stamina run of 8–12 miles at 7:45–8:15 per mile
- 2 endurance workouts on the track (select *one* of the following per workout):
  - 12 × 220 in :42; 440 R
  - 12 × 440 in :93; 220 R
  - 5 × 880 in 3:12; 440 R
  - 4 × 1 mile in 6:20; 660 R
  - 440 in :90; 880 in 3:10; ¾ mile in 4:55; ¾ mile in 4:50; 880 in 3:05; 440 in :88; all 440 R
- 1 medium-distance run (5–8 miles) at 7:00–7:45
- 3 days of medium-distance (5–8 miles) maintenance runs at 7:45–8:15 per mile

Two morning runs of 3 miles with 4 to 6 strides of 70 to 100 yards should also be included in the conditioning schedule.

In both the conditioning and specialized schedules, each track workout should begin with a 1- to 2-mile easy warm-up and end with a 1- to 2-mile easy warm-down. Also in both schedules, "R" means jog recovery unless otherwise specified; when "R" represents a time, the interval should be spent walking or resting.

"Easy running" in the eight-week specialized training schedule is 7:45 to 8:15 per mile.

## 1st Week

### Day

1   8 miles easy running
2   A.M. 3 miles easy running incorporating 6 × 100 (fast and controlled)
    P.M. 5 miles in 35:00
3   12 × 220 in :39; 440 R
4   A.M. 3 miles easy running incorporating 6 × 100 (fast and controlled)
    P.M. 3 miles easy running
5   6 × 880 in 2:55; 880 R
6   5 miles easy running
7   6 miles in 42:00

## 2nd Week

### Day

1   6 miles easy running incorporating 8 × 100 (fast and controlled)
2   A.M. 3 miles easy running
    P.M. 660 in 2:10; 110 R; 220 in :39; 550 R — repeat set 5 more times
3   6 miles in 42:00
4   A.M. 3 miles easy running incorporating 5 × 100 (fast and controlled)
    P.M. 3 miles easy running
5   A.M. 3 miles easy running incorporating 6 × 100 (fast and controlled)
    P.M. 4 miles easy running
6   6 miles easy running incorporating 3 miles in 19:00
7   6 miles in 42:00

## 3rd Week

### Day

1   12 × 330 in :60; 330 R
2   6 miles in 41:00
3   3 × 1¼ miles in 7:45; 660 R
4   A.M. 3 miles easy running incor-

porating 6 × 100 (fast and controlled)
    P.M. 3 miles easy running
5   8 × 440 in :77; 440 R
6   5 miles easy running
7   2-mile time trial *or* competitive effort at 1–2 miles

## 4th Week

### Day

1   8 miles easy running
2   A.M. 3 miles easy running incorporating 8 × 100 (fast and controlled)
    P.M. 6 miles in 42:00
3   6 miles easy running
4   A.M. 3 miles easy running incorporating 8 × 100 (fast and controlled)
    P.M. 6 miles easy running
5   4 × 1 mile in 6:15; 440 R
6   6 miles easy running
7   6 miles easy running incorporating 3 miles in 19:00

## 5th Week

### Day

1   6 miles easy running
2   12 × 440 in :90; 440 R
3   A.M. 3 miles easy running incorporating 6 × 100 (fast and controlled)
    P.M. 3 miles easy running
4   2 × 1½ miles in 9:30; 880 R
5   6 miles easy running incorporating 6 × 100 (fast and controlled)
6   2 × 1 mile in 5:45; 1 mile R
7   6 miles easy running

## 6th Week

### Day

1   10 miles in 70:00
2   A.M. 3 miles easy running incor-

porating 6 × 100 (fast and controlled)
P.M. 4 miles easy running

3    A.M. 3 miles easy running
P.M. 6 × 550 in 1:40; 660 R

4    2 × 1½ miles in 9:30; 880 R

5    5 miles easy running

6    Rest day

7    Competitive effort at 1–3 miles *or* 2 miles in 12:15

## 7th Week

*Day*

1    6 miles easy running

2    A.M. 3 miles easy running incorporating 5 × 100 (fast and controlled)
P.M. 3 × 1 mile in 6:05; 440 R

3    5 miles easy running

4    A.M. 3 miles easy running incorporating 10 × 100 (fast and controlled)
P.M. 4 miles easy running

5    5 miles easy running

6    6 miles easy running incorporating 4 miles in 26:00

7    8 × 440 in :78; 440 R

## 8th Week

*Day*

1    10 miles in 72:30

2    A.M. 3 miles easy running incorporating 6 × 100 (fast and controlled)
P.M. 5 × 880 in 2:55; 440 R

3    5 miles easy running

4    A.M. 3 miles easy running incorporating 5 × 100 (fast and controlled)
P.M. 3 miles easy running

5    Rest day

6    3 miles easy running

7    5K race in 19:00

*Peggy Smith, professor of medicine. (Photograph by Agapito San-chez)*

# The 20:00 5K
# The 19:19 3 Miles
# The 12:18 2 Miles

*You are ready to train for the above distances if you can run:*

*440 yards in 75 seconds*
*1 mile in 5:50*

*To run 5K in 20:00 and 3 miles in 19:19, you will need to average approximately 96.5 seconds per quarter*
*To run 2 miles in 12:18, you will need to average 92.25 seconds per quarter*

The recommended weekly mileage during the conditioning period is 40 to 45 miles. We suggest an eight-week conditioning program that contains the following elements in a typical week's training:

- 1 long stamina run of 7–10 miles at 8:00–8:30 per mile
- 2 endurance workouts on the track (select *one* of the following per workout):
  - 10 × 220 in :43; 440 R
  - 10 × 440 in :98; 220 R
  - 4 × 880 in 3:20; 440 R
  - 3 × 1 mile in 6:45; 880 R
  - 440 in :95; 880 in 3:15; ¾ mile in 5:05; ¾ mile in 5:05; 880 in 3:15; 440 in :95; all 440 R
- 1 medium-distance run (4–6 miles) at 7:15–8:00 per mile
- 3 days of medium-distance (4–6 miles) maintenance runs at 8:00–8:30 per mile

Two early morning runs per week during the conditioning period are optional. Each run should be 3 miles with 4 to 6 strides of 70 to 100 yards at a fast and controlled pace.

In both the conditioning and specialized schedules, each track workout should begin with a 1- to 2-mile easy warm-up and end with a 1- to 2-mile easy warm-down. Also in both schedules, "R" means jog recovery unless otherwise specified; when "R" represents a time, the interval should be spent walking or resting.

"Easy running" in this schedule is 8:00 to 8:30 per mile.

## 1st Week

*Day*

1   7 miles easy running
2   5 miles in 37:30
3   10 × 220 in :40; 440 R
4   A.M. 3 miles easy running incorporating 6 × 100 (fast and controlled)
    P.M. 3 miles easy running
5   5 × 880 in 3:10; 880 R
6   5 miles easy running
7   6 miles in 45:00

## 2nd Week

*Day*

1   5 miles easy running incorporating 8 × 100 (fast and controlled)
2   660 in 2:20; 110 R; 220 in :40; 550 R — repeat set 4 more times
3   5 miles easy running
4   6 miles in 45:00
5   A.M. 3 miles easy running incorporating 6 × 100 (fast and controlled)
    P.M. 3 miles easy running
6   6 miles easy running incorporating 3 miles in 20:00
7   6 miles in 45:00

## 3rd Week

*Day*

1   10 × 330 in :64; 330 R
2   6 miles easy running
3   3 × 1¼ miles in 8:05; 660 R
4   5 miles easy running
5   8 × 440 in :82; 440 R
6   4 miles easy running
7   2-mile time trial *or* competitive effort at 1–2 miles

## 4th Week

*Day*

1   6 miles easy running
2   5 miles in 36:15
3   6 miles easy running
4   A.M. 3 miles easy running incorporating 6 × 100 (fast and controlled)
    P.M. 4 miles easy running
5   4 × 1 mile in 6:45; 440 R
6   5 miles easy running
7   6 miles easy running incorporating 3 miles in 20:00

## 5th Week

*Day*

1   6 miles easy running
2   10 × 440 in :95; 440 R
3   A.M. 3 miles easy running incorporating 6 × 100 (fast and controlled)
    P.M. 4 miles easy running
4   2 × 1½ miles in 10:00; 880 R
5   5 miles easy running incorporating 5 × 100 (fast and controlled)
6   2 × 1 mile in 6:05; 1 mile R
7   4 miles easy running

## 6th Week

*Day*

1   8 miles in 58:00
2   A.M. 3 miles easy running incorporating 5 × 100 (fast and controlled)
    P.M. 3 miles easy running
3   6 × 550 in 1:42; 660 R
4   4 miles easy running
5   2 × 1½ miles in 10:00; 880 R
6   Rest day
7   Competitive effort at 1–3 miles *or* 2 miles in 13:00

## 7th Week

### Day

1  6 miles easy running
2  3 × 1 mile in 6:10; 440 R
3  5 miles easy running
4  6 miles easy running incorporating 8 × 100 (fast and controlled)
5  5 miles easy running
6  5 miles easy running incorporating 3 miles in 21:00
7  8 × 440 in :80; 440 R

## 8th Week

### Day

1  8 miles in 58:00
2  4 × 880 in 3:00; 440 R
3  5 miles easy running
4  5 miles easy running with 6 × 100 (fast and controlled)
5  Rest day
6  3 miles easy running
7  5K race in 20:00

Carol Gaye Castro, data processor. (Photograph by Bruce Glikin)

# The 21:00 5K
# The 20:17 3 Miles
# The 12:48 2 Miles

---

*You are ready to train for the above distances if you can run:*

*440 yards in 78 seconds*
*1 mile in 6:10*

*To run 5K in 21:00 and 3 miles in 20:17, you will need to average approximately 1:41.5 per quarter*
*To run 2 miles in 12:48, you will need to average 96 seconds per quarter*

---

The recommended weekly mileage during the eight-week conditioning period is 35 to 45 miles. The following elements should be included in a typical week's training:

- 1 long stamina run of 6–9 miles at 8:15–8:45 per mile
- 2 endurance workouts on the track (select *one* of the following per workout):
  - 10 × 220 in :44; 440 R
  - 8 × 440 in 1:40; 220 R
  - 4 × 880 in 3:25; 440 R
  - 3 × 1 mile in 7:10; 880 R
  - 440 in 1:40; 880 in 3:30; ¾ mile in 5:20; ¾ mile in 5:20; 880 in 3:30; 440 in :98; all 440 R
- 1 medium-distance run (4–6 miles) at 7:30–8:00 per mile
- 3 medium-distance (4–6 miles) maintenance runs at 8:15–8:45 per mile

In both the conditioning and specialized schedules, each track workout should begin with a 1- to 2-mile easy warm-up and end with a 1- to 2-mile easy warm-down. Also in both schedules, "R" means jog recovery unless otherwise specified; when "R" represents a time, the interval should be spent walking or resting.

"Easy running" in this schedule is 8:30 per mile.

## 1st Week

*Day*

1   6 miles easy running
2   5 miles in 38:45
3   10 × 220 in :42; 440 R
4   4 miles easy running
5   4 × 880 in 3:30; 880 R
6   5 miles easy running
7   5 miles in 38:45

## 2nd Week

*Day*

1   5 miles easy running incorporating 8 × 100 (fast and controlled)
2   660 in 2:25; 110 R; 220 in :42; 550 R — repeat set 3 more times
3   4 miles easy running
4   6 miles in 46:30
5   5 miles easy running incorporating 6 × 100 (fast and controlled)
6   4 miles easy running incorporating 3 miles in 21:45
7   5 miles in 38:45

## 3rd Week

*Day*

1   8 × 330 in :66; 330 R
2   5 miles easy running
3   3 × 1¼ miles in 8:30; 880 R
4   4 miles easy running
5   8 × 440 in :85; 440 R
6   4 miles easy running
7   Competitive effort at 1 or 2 miles *or* 2-mile time trial

## 4th Week

*Day*

1   6 miles easy running
2   5 miles in 38:45
3   5 miles easy running

4   5 miles easy running incorporating 6 × 100 (fast and controlled)
5   3 × 1 mile in 7:00; 440 R
6   4 miles easy running
7   5 miles easy running incorporating 3 miles in 20:30

## 5th Week

*Day*

1   6 miles easy running
2   8 × 440 in :95; 440 R
3   5 miles easy running incorporating 6 × 100 (fast and controlled)
4   2 × 1½ miles in 10:20; 880 R
5   4 miles easy running incorporating 5 × 100 (fast and controlled)
6   2 × 1 mile in 6:20; 1 mile R
7   4 miles easy running

## 6th Week

*Day*

1   8 miles in 62:00
2   4 miles easy running incorporating 6 × 100 (fast and controlled)
3   5 × 550 in 1:44; 660 R
4   4 miles easy running
5   2 × 1½ miles in 10:20; 880 R
6   Rest day
7   Competitive effort at 1–3 miles *or* 2 miles in 13:30

## 7th Week

*Day*

1   6 miles easy running
2   3 × 1 mile in 6:25; 440 R
3   5 miles easy running
4   4 miles easy running incorporating 6 × 100 (fast and controlled)
5   5 miles easy running

6  5 miles easy running incorporating 3 miles in 21:45

7  6 × 440 in :83; 440 R

## 8th Week

_Day_

1  8 miles in 62:00

2  3 × 880 in 3:10; 440 R

3  4 miles easy running

4  5 miles easy running incorporating 6 × 100 (fast and controlled)

5  Rest day

6  3 miles easy running

7  5K race in 21:00

*Surges incorporated in easy runs and track workouts can add greatly to a runner's racing ability. (Photograph by Bruce Glikin)*

# 5 Miles — 8 Kilometers

ALTHOUGH RARELY RUN TEN YEARS AGO, the 8K/5-mile race (the difference between the metric and the English measurement is less than 50 meters) has become increasingly popular among both race directors and runners. Its popularity stems from a number of reasons.

First, it is widely perceived as a "step-up" to the 10K. Although it is only 1.2 miles shorter, the 8K/5-mile distance provides an extra boost in confidence to those who look forward to training and competing at longer distances. (There have no doubt been many runners, in fact, who have wished that the 10K they were running were a mile shorter.) Additionally, the 5-mile race is frequently run in Corporate Cup road-race competitions since it serves as a good compromise between 5K and 10K races.

Finally, the 8K/5-mile distance can serve as a transitional event because it provides a good opportunity to apply some of the power-running techniques of shorter distances to events that are usually thought of as endurance races

Emil Zatopek's domination of distance running in the early 1950s was partly due to his ability to throw frequent fast surges at his opposition during a race. Although Zatopek usually ran "even splits" — each lap in the same time — his pace would vary during the lap. Once or twice per lap Zatopek would accelerate for 20 or 30 yards, offering his opponents the choice of letting him get away from them or of chancing oxygen debt before the final sprint for the tape.

My Australian coach, "Chicks" Hensley, felt that Zatopek's surging ability stemmed from training preparation rather than natural talent. Accordingly, we began incorporating a series of sharp 55-yard sprints into my regular 440-yard interval training sessions. At first we began with one per lap, but in several weeks we had built this to $2 \times 55$ yards in each 440. My improvement was significant: Not only did my best 10K time improve by two minutes in six months, but I found that I could use the surge as a devastating tactical tool.

In the last decade, male distance runners have improved so much at the international level that the surge has practically disappeared as a tactical weapon; instead, a runner who hopes to win has to run almost all out from the start and hope that he will outlast his competition. But while watching the women's 10K at the 1985 National Sports Festival, I was struck by how similar (in times and tactics) this race was to races I had run thirty years earlier on another continent.

Since 1985, I have incorporated the 50-meter sprint into the 400-meter workouts of many of my trainees. The results have ranged from average to spectacular in producing faster times, but most noticeable has been the ability of runners trained by this technique to respond to the challenge of a fast burst of speed in a race.

If you would like to introduce such surges into your workouts and thus take advantage of the short-distance training you have made use of in other chapters of the book, keep these rules in mind:

- start with one 50-meter surge in the middle of each lap
- work up to a maximum of two per lap
- don't start or end a lap with a surge — keep them in the middle of your effort (this trains you to accelerate from a given pace and return to it after your surge)

*Donald Speranza, Jr., sales representative. (Photograph by Sri Chinmoy Public Relations)*

# The 24:00 8K

*You are ready to train for a 24:00 8K if you can run:*

220 yards in 27 seconds
440 yards in 58 seconds
1 mile in 4:12

*To run 8K in 24:00, you will need to average 4:48 per mile*

In training for a 24-minute 8K, you should follow an initial eight-week conditioning program, running 60 to 80 miles weekly. A typical week's training during the conditioning period consists of:

- 1 long stamina run of 12–15 miles at 6:15–7:00 per mile
- 1 medium-distance run (7–10 miles) with 6–10 strides of 60–120 yards, run at a fast and controlled pace
- 3 days of medium-distance (7–10 miles) maintenance runs at 6:15–7:00 per mile
- 2 endurance workouts on the track
  - Short endurance (select *one* of the following per workout):
    16 × 110 in :15–:16; 110 R
    12 × 220 in :32–:33; 220 R
    10 × 330 in :50–:52; 220 R
    10 × 440 in :68–:70; 220 R
  - Medium endurance (select *one* of the following per workout):
    8 × 660 in 1:45–1:50; 440 R
    6 × 880 in 2:25–2:30; 440 R
    5 × ¾ mile in 3:45–3:50; 440 R

At this level of running, plan on three or four morning runs a week. These runs should cover 3 to 4½ miles with 4 to 8 fast and controlled strides of 60 to 120 yards incorporated. Morning running should continue during the conditioning and the specialized phase of this schedule.

In both the conditioning and specialized schedules, each track workout should begin with a 1- to 2-mile easy warm-up and end with a 1- to 2-mile easy warm-down. Also in both schedules, "R" means jog recovery unless otherwise specified; when "R" represents a time, the interval should be spent walking or resting.

After finishing the conditioning phase, you are ready to proceed with the eight weeks of specialized training leading to the 24-minute 8K.

"Easy running" in this schedule is 6:15 to 7:15 per mile.

## 1st Week

*Day*

1   15 miles easy running
2   440 in :70; 110 R; 110 in :15; 440 R — repeat set 9 more times
3   6 miles easy running
4   4 × 1 mile in 5:00; 880 R
5   8 miles easy running
6   10 miles in 57:30
7   6 miles easy running

## 2nd Week

*Day*

1   12 miles easy running incorporating 2 × 3 miles in 17:00
2   660 in 1:45; 110 R; 220 in :33; 550 R — repeat set 4 more times
3   6 miles easy running
4   1 mile in 4:45; ¾ mile in 3:30; 880 in 2:15; 660 R
5   6 miles easy running
6   9 miles easy running
7   10 miles in 57:30

## 3rd Week

*Day*

1   12 miles easy running
2   4 × 1 mile in 5:00; 440 R
3   6 miles in 36:00
4   4 × 880 in 2:18; 440 R
5   Rest day
6   6 miles easy running
7   Competitive effort at 5K–10K

## 4th Week

*Day*

1   12 miles easy running
2   16 × 110 in :15; 330 R
3   7 miles easy running incorporating 2 miles in 10:00
4   20 × 440 in :75; 440 R
5   6 miles easy running
6   6 miles easy running
7   10 miles in 55:00

## 5th Week

*Day*

1   15 miles easy running
2   3 × 330 in :45; 110 R; jog 880; 3 × 330 in :45; 110 R
3   6 miles easy running
4   6 × 880 in 2:15; 660 R
5   Rest day
6   6 miles easy running
7   Competitive effort at 5K–15K

## 6th Week

*Day*

1   12 miles easy running
2   10 × 220 in :31; 220 R
3   9 miles easy running
4   3 × 1¼ miles in 6:15; 440 R
5   6 miles easy running
6   6 miles in 34:00
7   10 miles easy running

## 7th Week

*Day*

1   12 miles easy running
2   440 in :68; 110 R; 110 in :15; 440 R — repeat set 7 more times
3   6 miles in 35:00
4   6 miles easy running
5   9 miles easy running incorporating 2 × 2 miles in 9:40
6   6 miles easy running
7   10 miles in 57:30

## 8th Week

*Day*

1   10 miles easy running
2   16 × 220 in :36; 110 R
3   6 miles easy running
4   3 × ¾ mile in 3:30; 440 R
5   Rest day
6   6 miles easy running
7   8K race in 24:00

*Bill Weaver, accountant. (Photograph by Hardy Meredith,* The Daily Sentinel, *Nacogdoches, Texas*)

# The 25:30 8K

*You are ready to train for a 25:30 8K if you can run:*

220 *yards in 28 seconds*
440 *yards in 60 seconds*
1 *mile in 4:28*

*To run 8K in 25:30, you will need to average 5:06 per mile*

To run 8K in 25:30, we recommend a conditioning period of eight weeks with a weekly mileage total of 60 to 80 miles. A typical week's training should include the following:

- 1 long stamina run of 12–15 miles at 6:30–7:15 per mile
- 1 medium-distance run (7–10 miles) with 6–10 strides of 60–120 yards, run at a fast and controlled pace
- 3 days of medium-distance (7–10 miles) maintenance runs at 6:30–7:15 per mile
- 2 endurance workouts on the track:
  - Short endurance (select *one* of the following per workout):
    16 × 110 in :16; 110 R
    12 × 220 in :33–:34; 220 R
    10 × 330 in :52–:54; 220 R
    10 × 440 in :70–:72; 220 R
  - Medium endurance (select *one* of the following per workout):
    8 × 660 in 1:48–1:52; 440 R
    6 × 880 in 2:30–2:35; 440 R
    5 × ¾ mile in 3:52–3:58; 440 R

Three or four morning runs of 3 to 4 miles with 4 to 8 controlled strides of 60 to 120 yards are recommended weekly for runners of this level during both the conditioning and specialized phases.

In both the conditioning and specialized schedules, each track workout should begin with a 1- to 2-mile easy warm-up and end with a 1- to 2-mile easy warm-down. Also in both schedules, "R" means jog recovery unless otherwise specified; when "R" represents a time, the interval should be spent walking or resting.

"Easy running" in the specialized schedule is 6:30 to 7:30 per mile.

## 1st Week

*Day*

1  15 miles easy running
2  440 in :72; 110 R; 110 in :16; 440 R — repeat set 9 more times
3  6 miles easy running
4  4 × 1 mile in 5:10; 880 R
5  6 miles easy running
6  10 miles in 60:00
7  6 miles easy running

## 2nd Week

*Day*

1  12 miles easy running incorporating 2 × 3 miles in 17:30
2  660 in 1:50; 110 R; 220 in :34; 550 R — repeat set 4 more times
3  6 miles easy running
4  1 mile in 5:00; ¾ mile in 3:38; 880 in 2:20; 660 R
5  6 miles easy running
6  9 miles easy running
7  10 miles in 60:00

## 3rd Week

*Day*

1  12 miles easy running
2  4 × 1 mile in 5:08; 440 R
3  6 miles in 37:30
4  4 × 880 in 2:23; 440 R
5  Rest day
6  5 miles easy running
7  Competitive effort at 5K–10K

## 4th Week

*Day*

1  12 miles easy running
2  16 × 110 in :16; 330 R
3  7 miles easy running incorporating 2 miles in 10:20
4  20 × 440 in :78; 440 R
5  6 miles easy running
6  4 miles easy running
7  10 miles in 57:30

## 5th Week

*Day*

1  15 miles easy running
2  3 × 330 in :47; 110 R; jog 880; 3 × 330 in :47; 110 R
3  6 miles easy running
4  6 × 880 in 2:20; 660 R
5  Rest day
6  5 miles easy running
7  Competitive effort at 5K–15K

## 6th Week

*Day*

1  12 miles easy running
2  10 × 220 in :33; 220 R
3  9 miles easy running
4  3 × 1¼ miles in 6:40; 440 R
5  6 miles easy running
6  6 miles in 35:00
7  10 miles easy running

## 7th Week

### Day

1  12 miles easy running
2  440 in :70; 110 R; 110 in :16; 440
   R — repeat set 7 more times
3  6 miles in 36:00
4  6 miles easy running
5  9 miles easy running incorporating 2 × 2 miles in 10:15
6  6 miles easy running
7  10 miles in 59:00

## 8th Week

### Day

1  10 miles easy running
2  16 × 220 in :38; 110 R
3  6 miles easy running
4  3 × ¾ mile in 3:45; 440 R
5  Rest day
6  6 miles easy running
7  8K race in 25:30

*Jenni Peters, university professor. (Photograph by Fred Miller, Jr.)*

# The 27:00 8K

*You are ready to train for a 27:00 8K if you can run:*

*220 yards in 29 seconds*
*440 yards in 64 seconds*
*1 mile in 4:48*

*To run a 27:00 8K, you will need to average 5:24 per mile*

You should total 55 to 70 miles a week during the eight-week conditioning period before the final eight weeks of specialized training leading to a 27-minute 8K. We also recommend three or four morning runs per week; these should be 3 or 4 miles with 4 to 8 strides at controlled speed for 60 to 120 yards. A typical week's training during the conditioning period consists of the following:

- 1 long stamina run of 12–15 miles at 6:45–7:30 per mile
- one medium-distance run (6–8 miles) with 6–10 strides of 60–120 yards, run at a fast and controlled pace
- 3 days of medium-distance (6–8 miles) maintenance runs at 6:45–7:30 per mile
- 2 endurance workouts on the track:
  - Short endurance (select *one* of the following per workout):
    16 × 110 in :17; 110 R
    12 × 220 in :35; 220 R
    8 × 330 in :55; 220 R
    8 × 440 in :73–:75; 220 R
  - Medium endurance (select *one* of the following per workout):
    6 × 660 in 1:54; 440 R
    5 × 880 in 2:36; 440 R
    4 × ¾ mile in 4:00–4:05; 440 R

In both the conditioning and specialized schedules, each track workout should begin with a 1- to 2-mile easy warm-up and end with a 1- to 2-mile easy warm-down. Also in both schedules, "R" means jog recovery unless otherwise specified; when "R" represents a time, the interval should be spent walking or resting.

"Easy running" in the specialized schedule is 6:45 to 7:30 per mile.

## 1st Week

### Day

1   13 miles easy running
2   440 in :74; 110 R; 110 in :17; 440 R — repeat set 9 more times
3   5 miles easy running
4   4 × 1 mile in 5:30; 880 R
5   6 miles easy running
6   10 miles in 62:30
7   6 miles easy running

## 2nd Week

### Day

1   10 miles easy running incorporating 2 × 3 miles in 18:00
2   660 in 1:52; 110 R; 220 in :35; 550 R — repeat set 4 more times
3   6 miles easy running
4   1 mile in 5:15; ¾ mile in 3:50; 880 in 2:26; 660 R
5   6 miles easy running
6   6 miles easy running
7   8 miles in 48:00

## 3rd Week

### Day

1   10 miles easy running
2   4 × 1 mile in 5:12; 660 R
3   6 miles in 39:00
4   4 × 880 in 2:30; 660 R
5   Rest day
6   4 miles easy running
7   Competitive effort at 5K–10K

## 4th Week

### Day

1   10 miles easy running
2   16 × 110 in :17; 330 R
3   6 miles easy running incorporating 2 miles in 10:45
4   20 × 440 in :80; 440 R
5   6 miles easy running
6   3 miles easy running
7   10 miles in 60:00

## 5th Week

### Day

1   13 miles easy running
2   3 × 330 in :49; 110 R; jog 880; 3 × 330 in :49; 110 R
3   6 miles easy running
4   6 × 880 in 2:26; 660 R
5   Rest day
6   4 miles easy running
7   Competitive effort at 5K–15K

## 6th Week

### Day

1   12 miles easy running
2   10 × 220 in :34; 220 R
3   6 miles easy running
4   3 × 1¼ miles in 6:55; 440 R
5   6 miles easy running
6   6 miles easy running incorporating 3 miles in 17:30
7   9 miles easy running

## 7th Week

### Day

1  12 miles easy running
2  440 in :72; 110 R; 110 in :17; 440 R — repeat set 7 more times
3  6 miles in 37:30
4  6 miles easy running
5  6 miles easy running incorporating 2 × 2 miles in 10:45
6  6 miles easy running
7  10 miles in 62:30

## 8th Week

### Day

1  9 miles easy running
2  12 × 220 in :39; 110 R
3  5 miles easy running
4  3 × ¾ mile in 4:00; 440 R
5  Rest day
6  5 miles easy running
7  8K race in 27:00

*Donna Burge-Roark, shoe company representative. (Photograph by Steve Loosley)*

# The 28:30 8K

*You are ready to train for a 28:30 8K if you can run:*

*220 yards in 30 seconds*
*440 yards in 66 seconds*
*1 mile in 5:08*

*To run 8K in 28:30, you will need to average 5:42 per mile*

To run 8K in 28:30, an eight-week conditioning program covering 55 to 70 miles weekly is recommended. A typical week's schedule should include the following:

- 1 long stamina run of 12–15 miles at 7:00–7:45 per mile
- 1 medium-distance run (6–8 miles) with 6–8 strides of 60–120 yards, run at a fast and controlled pace
- 3 days of medium-distance (6–8 miles) maintenance runs at 7:00–7:45 per mile
- 2 endurance workouts on the track:
  - Short endurance (select *one* of the following per workout):
    16 × 110 in :17.5; 110 R
    12 × 220 in :36; 220 R
    8 × 330 in :56; 220 R
    6 × 440 in :76–:78; 220 R
  - Medium endurance (select *one* of the following per workout):
    6 × 660 in 2:00; 440 R
    5 × 880 in 2:40; 440 R
    4 × ¾ mile in 4:15; 440 R

Two or three morning runs of 3 miles with 6 strides of 60 to 120 yards at a fast and controlled pace would also be an advantage at this level of running.

In both the conditioning and specialized schedules, each track workout should begin with a 1- to 2-mile easy warm-up and end with a 1- to 2-mile easy warm-down. Also in both schedules, "R" means jog recovery unless otherwise specified; when "R" represents a time, the interval should be spent walking or resting.

"Easy running" in this schedule is 7:00 to 7:45 per mile.

## 1st Week

### Day

1  12 miles easy running
2  440 in :76; 110 R; 110 in :17.5; 440 R — repeat set 7 more times
3  5 miles easy running
4  4 × 1 mile in 5:40; 880 R
5  5 miles easy running
6  8 miles in 52:00
7  6 miles easy running

## 2nd Week

### Day

1  10 miles easy running incorporating 2 × 3 miles in 18:45
2  660 in 1:55; 110 R; 220 in :37; 550 R — repeat set 3 more times
3  6 miles easy running
4  1 mile in 5:25; ¾ mile in 4:00; 880 in 2:32; 880 R
5  5 miles easy running
6  6 miles easy running
7  8 miles in 50:00

## 3rd Week

### Day

1  10 miles easy running
2  4 × 1 mile in 5:30; 660 R
3  6 miles in 40:00
4  4 × 880 in 2:35; 660 R
5  Rest day
6  4 miles easy running
7  Competitive effort at 5K–10K

## 4th Week

### Day

1  10 miles easy running
2  16 × 110 in :17.5; 330 R
3  6 miles easy running incorporating 2 miles in 11:15
4  16 × 440 in :82; 440 R
5  6 miles easy running
6  3 miles easy running
7  10 miles in 62:30

## 5th Week

### Day

1  13 miles easy running
2  3 × 330 in :52; 110 R; jog 880; 3 × 330 in :52; 110 R
3  6 miles easy running
4  5 × 880 in 2:32; 880 R
5  Rest day
6  4 miles easy running
7  Competitive effort at 5K–15K

## 6th Week

### Day

1  12 miles easy running
2  10 × 220 in :35; 220 R
3  6 miles easy running
4  3 × 1¼ miles in 7:15; 440 R
5  6 miles easy running
6  6 miles easy running incorporating 3 miles in 18:00
7  9 miles easy running

## 7th Week

### Day

1   12 miles easy running
2   440 in :74; 110 R; 110 in :17 —
    repeat set 5 more times
3   6 miles in 39:00
4   6 miles easy running
5   6 miles easy running incorporat-
    ing 2 × 2 miles in 11:15
6   6 miles easy running
7   10 miles in 65:00

## 8th Week

### Day

1   9 miles easy running
2   10 × 220 in :39; 110 R
3   5 miles easy running
4   3 × ¾ mile in 4:15; 440 R
5   Rest day
6   4 miles easy running
7   8K race in 28:30

*Catherine Duncan, health and physical education teacher. (Photograph by Bruce Glikin)*

# The 30:00 8K

*You are ready to train for a 30:00 8K if you can run:*

220 *yards in 32 seconds*
440 *yards in 68 seconds*
1 *mile in 5:15*

*To run 8K in 30:00, you will need to average 6:00 per mile*

An eight-week conditioning period of 50 to 65 miles weekly is recommended before the final eight weeks of specialized training. A typical week's schedule during the conditioning phase should contain:

- 1 long stamina run of 10–13 miles at 7:15–8:00 per mile
- 1 medium-distance run (5–7 miles) with 6–8 strides of 60–120 yards, run at a fast and controlled pace
- 3 days of medium-distance (5–7 miles) maintenance runs at 7:15–8:00 per mile
- 2 endurance workouts on the track
  - Short endurance (select *one* of the following per workout):
    16 × 110 in :18.5; 110 R
    10 × 220 in :38; 220 R
    6 × 330 in :56; 220 R
    6 × 440 in :78–:80; 220 R
  - Medium endurance (select *one* of the following per workout):
    6 × 660 in 2:06; 440 R
    4 × 880 in 2:45; 440 R
    4 × ¾ mile in 4:20; 440 R

In both the conditioning and specialized schedules, each track workout should begin with a 1- to 2-mile easy warm-up and end with a 1- to 2-mile easy warm-down. Also in both schedules, "R" means jog recovery unless otherwise specified; when "R" represents a time, the interval should be spent walking or resting.

"Easy running" in the specialized eight-week schedule is 7:15 to 8:00 per mile.

## 1st Week

*Day*

1   10 miles easy running
2   440 in :78; 110 R; 110 in :18; 440 R — repeat set 7 more times
3   5 miles easy running
4   4 × 1 mile in 5:45; 660 R
5   5 miles easy running
6   8 miles in 54:00
7   6 miles easy running

## 2nd Week

*Day*

1   10 miles easy running incorporating 2 × 3 miles in 19:30
2   660 in 2:00; 110 R; 220 in :39; 550 R — repeat set 3 more times
3   6 miles easy running
4   1 mile in 5:35; ¾ mile in 4:05; 880 in 2:38; all 880 R
5   5 miles easy running
6   5 miles easy running
7   8 miles in 52:00

## 3rd Week

*Day*

1   10 miles easy running
2   4 × 1 mile in 5:38; 660 R
3   6 miles in 41:00
4   4 × 880 in 2:40; 660 R
5   Rest day
6   4 miles easy running
7   Competitive effort at 5K–10K

## 4th Week

*Day*

1   10 miles easy running
2   16 × 110 in :18; 330 R
3   6 miles easy running incorporating 2 miles in 11:30
4   16 × 440 in :84; 440 R
5   6 miles easy running
6   3 miles easy running
7   8 miles in 52:00

## 5th Week

*Day*

1   13 miles easy running
2   3 × 330 in :54; 110 R; jog 880; 3 × 330 in :54; 110 R
3   6 miles easy running
4   5 × 880 in 2:38; 880 R
5   Rest day
6   4 miles easy running
7   Competitive effort at 5K–15K

## 6th Week

*Day*

1   12 miles easy running
2   10 × 220 in :37; 220 R
3   6 miles easy running
4   3 × 1¼ miles in 7:20; 660 R
5   6 miles easy running
6   6 miles easy running incorporating 3 miles in 19:00
7   7 miles easy running

## 7th Week

### Day

1   10 miles easy running
2   440 in :76; 110 R; 110 in :18; 440
    R — repeat set 5 more times
3   6 miles in 40:00
4   6 miles easy running
5   6 miles easy running incorporat-
    ing 2 × 2 miles in 11:30
6   6 miles easy running
7   10 miles in 67:30

## 8th Week

### Day

1   8 miles easy running
2   10 × 220 in :40; 110 R
3   5 miles easy running
4   3 × ¾ mile in 4:20; 440 R
5   Rest day
6   4 miles easy running
7   8K race in 30:00

*Donald Baxter, orthopedic surgeon. (Photograph by Frances Baxter)*

# The 32:00 8K

*You are ready to train for a 32:00 8K if you can run:*

*220 yards in 34 seconds*
*440 yards in 72 seconds*
*1 mile in 5:30*

*To run 8K in 32:00, you will need to average 6:24 per mile*

An eight-week conditioning program of 45 to 60 miles weekly is recommended for this standard. A typical week's program should contain:

- 1 long stamina run of 10–13 miles at 7:30–8:15 per mile
- 1 medium-distance run (4–6 miles) with 4–8 strides of 60–120 yards, run at a fast and controlled pace
- 3 days of medium-distance (4–6 miles) maintenance runs at 7:30–8:15 per mile
- 2 endurance workouts on the track
  - Short endurance (select *one* of the following per workout):
    16 × 110 in :19; 110 R
    10 × 220 in :40; 220 R
    6 × 330 in :58; 220 R
    6 × 440 in :82; 220 R
  - Medium endurance (select *one* of the following per workout):
    6 × 660 in 2:12; 440 R
    4 × 880 in 2:50; 440 R
    4 × ¾ mile in 4:25; 440 R

In both the conditioning and specialized schedules, each track workout should begin with a 1- to 2-mile easy warm-up and end with a 1- to 2-mile easy warm-down. Also in both schedules, "R" means jog recovery unless otherwise specified; when "R" represents a time, the interval should be spent walking or resting.

"Easy running" in the specialized eight-week schedule is 7:30 to 8:15 per mile.

## 1st Week

### Day

1. 10 miles easy running
2. 440 in :82; 110 R; 110 in :18.5; 440 R — repeat set 7 more times
3. 5 miles easy running
4. 3 × 1 mile in 5:50; 660 R
5. 5 miles easy running
6. 8 miles in 56:00
7. 6 miles easy running

## 2nd Week

### Day

1. 8 miles easy running incorporating 2 × 3 miles in 20:00
2. 660 in 2:06; 110 R; 220 in :40; 550 R — repeat set 3 more times
3. 6 miles easy running
4. 1 mile in 5:50; ¾ mile in 4:12; 880 in 2:44; all 880 R
5. 5 miles easy running
6. 5 miles easy running
7. 8 miles in 54:00

## 3rd Week

### Day

1. 10 miles easy running
2. 3 × 1 mile in 5:50; 660 R
3. 6 miles in 42:00
4. 4 × 880 in 2:50; 660 R
5. Rest day
6. 3 miles easy running
7. Competitive effort at 5K–10K

## 4th Week

### Day

1. 8 miles easy running
2. 16 × 110 in :19; 330 R
3. 6 miles easy running incorporating 2 miles in 12:00
4. 12 × 440 in :88; 440 R
5. 6 miles easy running
6. 3 miles easy running
7. 8 miles in 54:00

## 5th Week

### Day

1. 12 miles easy running
2. 3 × 330 in :56; 110 R; jog 880; 3 × 330 in :56; 110 R
3. 5 miles easy running
4. 4 × 880 in 2:50; 880 R
5. Rest day
6. 4 miles easy running
7. Competitive effort at 5K–15K

## 6th Week

### Day

1. 10 miles easy running
2. 10 × 220 in :40; 220 R
3. 5 miles easy running
4. 3 × 1¼ miles in 8:00; 880 R
5. 5 miles easy running
6. 6 miles easy running incorporating 3 miles in 20:00
7. 6 miles easy running

## 7th Week

*Day*

1   10 miles easy running
2   440 in :82; 110 R; 110 in :19; 440
    R — repeat set 5 more times
3   5 miles in 34:00
4   5 miles easy running
5   6 *miles easy running incor-*
    *porating* 2 × 2 miles in 12:30
6   5 miles easy running
7   10 miles in 70:00

## 8th Week

*Day*

1   6 miles easy running
2   8 × 220 in :40; 110 R
3   5 miles easy running
4   2 × ¾ mile in 4:22; 880 R
5   Rest day
6   4 miles easy running
7   8K race in 32:00

*John Egan, former professional basketball player, and Joan Egan, homemaker. (Photograph by Bob Schneider)*

# The 34:00 8K

*You are ready to train for a 34:00 8K if you can run:*

*220 yards in 36 seconds*
*440 yards in 76 seconds*
*1 mile in 5:45*

*To run 8K in 34:00, you will need to average 6:48 per mile*

An eight-week conditioning program of 40 to 50 miles weekly is required for this standard. A typical week's program should contain:

- 1 long stamina run of 9–12 miles at 7:45–8:30 per mile
- 1 medium-distance run (4–6 miles) with 4–8 strides of 60–120 yards, run at a fast and controlled pace
- 3 days of medium-distance (4–6 miles) maintenance runs at 7:45–8:30 per mile
- 2 endurance workouts on the track:
  - Short endurance (select *one* of the following per workout):
    12 × 110 in :20; 110 R
    8 × 220 in :42; 220 R
    6 × 330 in :60; 330 R
    5 × 440 in :84; 220 R
  - Medium endurance (select *one* of the following per workout):
    5 × 660 in 2:15; 660 R
    4 × 880 in 3:00; 660 R
    3 × ¾ mile in 4:35; 660 R

In both the conditioning and specialized schedules, each track workout should begin with a 1- to 2-mile easy warm-up and end with a 1- to 2-mile easy warm-down. Also in both schedules, "R" means jog recovery unless otherwise specified; when "R" represents a time, the interval should be spent walking or resting.

"Easy running" in the specialized schedule is 7:45 to 8:30 per mile.

## 1st Week

### Day

1   10 miles easy running
2   440 in :84; 110 R; 110 in :20; 440
    R — repeat set 7 more times
3   4 miles easy running
4   3 × 1 mile in 6:00; 880 R
5   5 miles easy running
6   8 miles in 58:00
7   6 miles easy running

## 2nd Week

### Day

1   8 miles easy running incorporat-
    ing 2 × 2 miles in 14:30
2   660 in 2:15; 110 R; 220 in :42;
    550 R — repeat set 3 more times
3   5 miles easy running
4   1 mile in 5:55; ¾ mile in 4:18;
    880 in 2:48; all 880 R
5   5 miles easy running
6   5 miles easy running
7   8 miles in 58:00

## 3rd Week

### Day

1   8 miles easy running
2   3 × 1 mile in 6:00; 880 R
3   6 miles in 45:00
4   3 × 880 in 2:52; 880 R
5   Rest day
6   3 miles easy running
7   Competitive effort at 5K–10K

## 4th Week

### Day

1   6 miles easy running
2   16 × 110 in :20; 330 R
3   5 miles easy running incorporat-
    ing 2 miles in 13:00
4   10 × 440 in :92; 440 R
5   5 miles easy running
6   3 miles easy running
7   6 miles in 43:00

## 5th Week

### Day

1   10 miles easy running
2   3 × 330 in :60; 110 R; jog 880;
    3 × 330 in :60; 110 R
3   5 miles easy running
4   3 × 880 in 2:53; 880 R
5   Rest day
6   3 miles easy running
7   Competitive effort at 5K–15K

## 6th Week

### Day

1   10 miles easy running
2   10 × 220 in :42; 220 R
3   4 miles easy running
4   3 × 1¼ miles in 8:30; 880 R
5   5 miles easy running
6   5 miles easy running incorporat-
    ing 3 miles in 20:30
7   5 miles easy running

## 7th Week

### Day

1   8 miles easy running
2   440 in :84; 110 R; 110 in :20; 440
    R — repeat set 5 more times
3   5 miles in 35:00
4   5 miles easy running
5   5 miles easy running incorporat-
    ing 2 miles in 13:00
6   5 miles easy running
7   7 miles in 50:45

## 8th Week

### Day

1   6 miles easy running
2   8 × 220 in :42; 110 R
3   5 miles easy running
4   2 × 880 in 2:52; 880 R
5   Rest day
6   3 miles easy running
7   8K race in 34:00

*Danya Ellinor, marketing executive. (Photograph by Bruce Glikin)*

# The 36:00 8K

*You are ready to train for a 36:00 8K if you can run:*

*220 yards in 37 seconds*
*440 yards in 79 seconds*
*1 mile in 6:05*

*To run 8K in 36:00, you will need to average 7:12 per mile*

To run 8K in 36 minutes, we recommend an eight-week conditioning program of 35 to 45 miles weekly. A typical week's training during this period should contain:

- 1 long stamina run of 8–12 miles at 8:00–8:45 per mile
- 1 medium-distance run (4–6 miles) with 4–8 strides of 60–120 yards, run at a fast and controlled pace
- 3 days of medium-distance (4–6 miles) maintenance runs at 8:00–8:45 per mile
- 2 endurance workouts on the track
  - Short endurance (select *one* of the following per workout):
    12 × 110 in :21; 110 R
    8 × 220 in :43; 220 R
    5 × 330 in :62; 330 R
    5 × 440 in :86; 330 R
  - Medium endurance (select *one* of the following per workout):
    4 × 660 in 2:18; 660 R
    4 × 880 in 3:20; 660 R
    3 × ¾ mile in 4:50; 880 R

In both the conditioning and specialized schedules, each track workout should begin with a 1- to 2-mile easy warm-up and end with a 1- to 2-mile easy warm-down. Also in both schedules, "R" means jog recovery unless otherwise specified; when "R" represents a time, the interval should be spent walking or resting.

"Easy running" in this schedule is 8:00 to 8:45 per mile.

## 1st Week

### Day

1  8 miles easy running
2  440 in :86; 110 R; 110 in :21; 440 R — repeat set 7 more times
3  4 miles easy running
4  3 × 1 mile in 6:25; 880 R
5  4 miles easy running
6  6 miles in 48:00
7  5 miles easy running

## 2nd Week

### Day

1  6 miles easy running incorporating 2 × 2 miles in 15:00
2  660 in 2:18; 110 R; 220 in :44; 550 R — repeat set 3 more times
3  4 miles easy running
4  1 mile in 6:15; ¾ mile in 4:35; 880 in 2:55; all 880 R
5  5 miles easy running
6  5 miles easy running
7  6 miles in 47:00

## 3rd Week

### Day

1  7 miles easy running
2  3 × 1 mile in 6:20; 880 R
3  6 miles in 46:30
4  Rest day
5  3 × 880 in 3:05; 880 R
6  3 miles easy running
7  Competitive effort at 5K–10K

## 4th Week

### Day

1  6 miles easy running
2  12 × 110 in :21; 330 R
3  5 miles easy running incorporating 2 miles in 13:30
4  8 × 440 in :94; 440 R
5  4 miles easy running
6  4 miles easy running
7  6 miles in 46:30

## 5th Week

### Day

1  8 miles easy running
2  3 × 330 in :62; 220 R; jog 880; 3 × 330 in :62; 220 R
3  5 miles easy running
4  3 × 880 in 3:00; 880 R
5  Rest day
6  3 miles easy running
7  Competitive effort at 5K–15K

## 6th Week

### Day

1  9 miles easy running
2  8 × 220 in :43; 330 R
3  4 miles easy running
4  3 × 1¼ miles in 9:00; 880 R
5  4 miles easy running
6  4 miles easy running incorporating 2 miles in 13:30
7  5 miles easy running

## 7th Week

### Day

1  440 in :86; 110 R; 110 in :21; 440 R — repeat set 5 more times
2  5 miles in 37:30
3  4 miles easy running
4  5 miles easy running incorporating 2 × 1 mile in 7:30
5  4 miles easy running
6  5 miles easy running
7  6 miles in 47:00

## 8th Week

### Day

1  5 miles easy running
2  8 × 220 in :43; 220 R
3  5 miles easy running
4  2 × 880 in 3:00; 880 R
5  Rest day
6  3 miles easy running
7  8K race in 36:00

*Roy Cullen, executive. (Photograph by National Sports Photo)*

# The 38:00 8K

*You are ready to train for a 38:00 8K if you can run:*

*220 yards in 38 seconds*
*440 yards in 82 seconds*
*1 mile in 6:30*

*To run 8K in 38:00, you will need to average 7:36 per mile*

We recommend an eight-week conditioning program of 35 to 45 miles weekly before you begin the final eight-week specialized training program leading to an 8K in 38 minutes. A typical week's schedule during this conditioning phase should contain:

- 1 long stamina run of 8–12 miles at 8:15–9:00 per mile
- 1 medium-distance run (4–6 miles) with 4–8 strides of 60–120 yards, run at a fast and controlled pace
- 3 days of medium-distance (4–6 miles) maintenance runs at 8:15–9:00 per mile
- 2 endurance workouts on the track
  - Short endurance (select *one* of the following per workout):
    12 × 110 in :21.5; 110 R
    8 × 220 in :44; 220 R
    5 × 330 in :68; 330 R
    5 × 440 in :88; 440 R
  - Medium endurance (select *one* of the following per workout):
    4 × 660 in 2:30; 660 R
    4 × 880 in 3:30; 660 R
    3 × ¾ mile in 5:15; 880 R

For both the conditioning and specialized schedules, each track workout should begin with a 1- to 2-mile easy warm-up and end with a 1- to 2-mile easy warm-down. Also in both schedules, "R" means jog recovery unless otherwise specified; when "R" represents a time, the interval should be spent walking or resting.

"Easy running" in the specialized schedule is 8:15 to 9:00 per mile.

## 1st Week

### Day

1. 8 miles easy running
2. 440 in :88; 110 R; 110 in :21.5; 440 R — repeat set 7 more times
3. 4 miles easy running
4. 3 × 1 mile in 7:00; 880 R
5. 4 miles easy running
6. 6 miles in 49:30
7. 5 miles easy running

## 2nd Week

### Day

1. 6 miles easy running incorporating 2 × 2 miles in 15:30
2. 660 in 2:30; 110 R; 220 in :45; 550 R — repeat set 3 more times
3. 4 miles easy running
4. 1 mile in 6:50; ¾ mile in 5:00; 880 in 3:10; all 880 R
5. 5 miles easy running
6. 5 miles easy running
7. 6 miles in 49:30

## 3rd Week

### Day

1. 7 miles easy running
2. 3 × 1 mile in 6:50; 880 R
3. 6 miles in 49:30
4. Rest day
5. 3 × 880 in 3:10; 880 R
6. 3 miles easy running
7. Competitive effort at 5K–10K

## 4th Week

### Day

1. 6 miles easy running
2. 12 × 110 in :21.5; 330 R
3. 5 miles easy running incorporating 2 miles in 15:00
4. 8 × 440 in :96; 440 R
5. 4 miles easy running
6. 4 miles easy running
7. 6 miles in 49:30

## 5th Week

### Day

1. 8 miles easy running
2. 3 × 330 in :66; 220 R; jog 880; 3 × 330 in :66; 220 R
3. 5 miles easy running
4. 3 × 880 in 3:10; 880 R
5. Rest day
6. 3 miles easy running
7. Competitive effort at 5K–15K

## 6th Week

### Day

1. 9 miles easy running
2. 8 × 220 in :45; 330 R
3. 4 miles easy running
4. 4 × ¾ mile in 5:15; 880 R
5. 3 miles easy running
6. 4 miles easy running incorporating 2 miles in 15:00
7. 5 miles easy running

## 7th Week

*Day*

1   440 in :88; 110 R; 110 in :21.5; 440 R — repeat set 5 more times
2   5 miles in 40:00
3   4 miles easy running
4   5 miles easy running incorporating 2 × 1 mile in 7:45
5   5 miles easy running
6   4 miles easy running
7   6 miles in 49:30

## 8th Week

*Day*

1   5 miles easy running
2   8 × 220 in :45; 330 R
3   5 miles easy running
4   2 × 880 in 3:15; 880 R
5   Rest Day
6   3 miles easy running
7   8K race in 38:00

Nancy Bradley-Kelly, stockbroker. (Photograph by Howard Castle-
berry)

# The 40:00 8K

*You are ready to train for a 40:00 8K if you can run:*

220 *yards in 40 seconds*
440 *yards in 85 seconds*
1 *mile in 7:00*

*To run 8K in 40:00, you will need to average 8:00 per mile*

We recommend an eight-week conditioning program of 35 to 45 miles per week before the final eight weeks of specialized training. A typical week's training during the conditioning phase should include:

- 1 long stamina run of 8–12 miles at 8:30–9:15 per mile
- 1 medium-distance run (4–6 miles) with 4–8 strides of 60–120 yards, run at a fast and controlled pace
- 3 days of medium-distance (4–6 miles) maintenance runs at 8:30–9:15 per mile
- 2 endurance workouts on the track
  - Short endurance (select *one* of the following per workout):
    12 × 110 in :22; 110 R
    8 × 220 in :46; 220 R
    5 × 330 in :73; 330 R
    5 × 440 in :93; 440 R
  - Medium endurance (select *one* of the following per workout):
    4 × 660 in 2:45; 660 R
    4 × 880 in 3:45; 880 R
    3 × ¾ mile in 5:40; 880 R

For both the conditioning and specialized schedules, each track workout should begin with a 1- to 2-mile easy warm-up and end with a 1- to 2-mile easy warm-down. Also in both schedules, "R" means jog recovery unless otherwise specified; when "R" represents a time, the interval should be spent walking or resting.

"Easy running" in the specialized schedule is 8:30 to 9:15 per mile.

## 1st Week

### Day

1   8 miles easy running
2   440 in :92; 110 R; 110 in :22; 440 R — repeat set 7 more times
3   4 miles easy running
4   3 × 1 mile in 7:20; 880 R
5   4 miles easy running
6   6 miles in 51:00
7   5 miles easy running

## 2nd Week

### Day

1   6 miles easy running incorporating 3 miles in 25:00
2   660 in 2:45; 110 R; 220 in :46; 550 R — repeat set 3 more times
3   4 miles easy running
4   1 mile in 7:20; ¾ mile in 5:20; 880 in 3:40; all 880 R
5   5 miles easy running
6   5 miles easy running
7   6 miles in 51:00

## 3rd Week

### Day

1   7 miles easy running
2   3 × 1 mile in 7:20; 880 R
3   6 miles in 51:00
4   Rest day
5   3 × 880 in 3:40; 880 R
6   3 miles easy running
7   Competitive effort at 5K–10K

## 4th Week

### Day

1   6 miles easy running
2   12 × 110 in :22; 330 R
3   4 miles easy running incorporating 2 miles in 16:00
4   8 × 440 in :98; 440 R
5   4 miles easy running
6   4 miles easy running
7   6 miles in 51:00

## 5th Week

### Day

1   8 miles easy running
2   3 × 330 in :72; 220 R; jog 880; 3 × 330 in :72; 220 R
3   5 miles easy running
4   3 × 880 in 3:30; 880 R
5   Rest day
6   3 miles easy running
7   Competitive effort at 5K–15K

## 6th Week

### Day

1   9 miles easy running
2   8 × 220 in :46; 330 R
3   4 miles easy running
4   4 × ¾ mile in 5:25; 880 R
5   3 miles easy running
6   4 miles easy running incorporating 2 miles in 16:00
7   5 miles easy running

## 7th Week

### Day

1. 440 in :90; 110 R; 110 in :22; 440 R — repeat set 5 more times
2. 5 miles in 42:30
3. 4 miles easy running
4. 5 miles easy running incorporating 2 × 1 mile in 8:00
5. 5 miles easy running
6. 4 miles easy running
7. 6 miles in 51:00

## 8th Week

### Day

1. 5 miles easy running
2. 8 × 220 in :46; 330 R
3. 5 miles easy running
4. 2 × 880 in 3:30; 880 R
5. Rest day
6. 3 miles easy running
7. 8K race in 40:00

*Lee Evans, holder of the oldest world record in track (400 meters in 43.86 seconds, set in 1968), shows the tremendous force generated in indoor curve running. (Photograph by Don Chadez; courtesy* Track and Field News)

# EIGHT

# Indoor Running

DURING THE LAST DECADE, indoor track competition has evolved from being restricted and elitist to being increasingly popular and widely available to all segments of the running population. Although the major U.S. indoor meets still cater to top national and international athletes, there is a steadily growing number of sites and meets available for high school, college, master's, and corporate competition.

Indoor track racing has unique benefits, and we feel that all self-coached runners at some point in their careers should include some indoor competition. All running is a learning experience, and some of the courses taught on the indoor track are especially valuable:

- Tight turns and small tracks will help you learn to compete in close quarters with your opponents.
- As a result of that, you will explore the tactical advantages of "running from the front."
- A controlled climate removes wind and temperature from the variables affecting performance.
- You will enjoy great spectator support, due to the closeness of the fans to the racing (although the presence of smoke and/or "not enough oxygen for so many people" may affect your racing).
- Your curve-running form will improve.

# Indoor Running
## Technique and Strategy

Curves can be a special problem in indoor running. In the first place, indoor tracks always have more laps to the mile, as few as five on a few "oversized" tracks to as many as twelve on others. The two most common sizes are eight or eleven laps to the mile, as compared with the standard outdoor track of four laps to the mile. That means that, automatically, the number of curves at any given event is at least doubled — for example, a half-mile (which has four curves outdoors) has from eight to eleven on an indoor track; a 3-mile racer may have sixty-six curves to negotiate.

Second, curves in indoor tracks are usually tighter because of the limited space available. An indoor racer thus has not only more turns to run but harder turns, too. The curves may be banked to offset a runner's inertia and to "hold him on the track" as he speeds around the bend, adding another complication not faced by the outdoor competitor.

Finally, while outdoor tracks are as a rule either asphalt or synthetic, a runner in an indoor meet may find herself on concrete, wooden blocks, plywood over wooden struts, plywood with rubberized material on top, boards nailed lengthwise to cross-joists, or the latest synthetic track material.

Thus even an experienced track racer may feel himself in the twilight zone when he ventures onto an indoor track for the first time. The key to successful indoor racing is to turn the peculiarities of an indoor facility into the strengths that will help you overcome your competitors. In indoor running, this means, first and foremost, that you need to become a superior curve runner.

In Washington, D.C., in 1959, I lined up for my first indoor race. The track had eight unbanked laps to the mile. I struggled through the curves and finished a disappointing sixth out of eight runners. Two weeks later I had another bad race on an eleven-lap-per-mile board track at Madison Square Garden. Compounding my poor showing, the sharp curves had caused a number of deep blisters on both soles and these split open whenever I ran faster than a jog in training.

Although I loved the general atmosphere of indoor competition and the closeness of the fans to the action, I finally went to my coach, John Morriss, and asked to forgo the rest of the indoor season. I told him that I just couldn't handle the "boards" — especially the curves.

My coach agreed with me but suggested that I should honor my commitments to run in two late-season meets, unless I felt that I was injured so severely that I was physically unable to compete. He gave me two weeks of grass running to allow my feet to heal, and before we left for New York and the finale of my "indoor career," he brought me into his office for a quiet talk.

"Al," he said, "first I want you to know that there's nothing wrong with your training or your present condition. You seem 'tight' when you run the curves, but you've got to realize that there is not much difference between an indoor and an outdoor curve — it's just a question of degree. You've been running like a crab running sideways, and you've got to learn to relax and run around them without fighting them. Respect them, but don't fear them."

After I left his office and looked back on his talk, I realized that he was right. I could see that I had been overreacting to what I perceived as the uniqueness of indoor curves. My method of running them had been to drop my left arm and drive my right arm across my body while turning my upper body toward the center of the arena. This curve technique had undoubtedly caused my feet to turn inward, creating tremendous friction on my soles. I was certain I had discovered the reason for my poor indoor showing.

Before I lined up for the AAU National Indoor 3-Mile Championship, the great Villanova coach Jumbo Elliott came up to me and said, "Al, you will do well — if you just relax and run the curves!" To this day I don't know whether this advice was a result of his own observations or whether my own shrewd coach had asked him to talk to me. I like to think that this great coach and gentleman offered his advice unsolicited to a runner who was having trouble adjusting to indoor competition.

That night I had a great race, leading for thirty-two of the thirty-three laps. Bill Dellinger's race was even better, as he kicked past me on the back straight to set a new world indoor record. The curves proved to be no problem, and I was able to relax (without slowing the pace) for the first time in an indoor race.

Six days later I ran alone from the start and broke the 2-mile world

*Allan Lawrence relaxing on the way to his indoor 2-mile world record, 1960. (Photograph by Larry Sharkey,* Los Angeles Times*)*

indoor record at the Knights of Columbus Meet at Madison Square Garden. The following season I was able to add the indoor 3-mile world record and finish the year undefeated. So, relax the curves; they're not as strange as they seem at first, and once you master them you can make them into a strength.

## INDOOR TACTICS

In some ways tactics are not as critical in indoor distance competition, because a major outdoor consideration is missing: wind. As a result, the front-running tactic becomes an extremely useful weapon to have at your disposal. A natural front-runner plying his trade in indoor competition is particularly dangerous, because the wind plays no part in contributing to his eventual fatigue. As a bonus, the front-runner has free and unimpeded running ahead of those who must fight it out in the pack for position on the narrow track. Even if you are not a natural front-runner, you can practice this tactic in indoor races and so develop a wider range of tactical experience than you can get outdoors.

To make the front-running technique especially effective, a runner can include sprints and acceleration drills in his regular training routine and develop his ability to surge away from opponents in a distance race. Surging is effective in securing a break for the front-runner — or, just as important, in weakening an opponent so that he has no kick at the end of an event.

If an athlete is particularly diligent in mastering this tactic, he will soon develop the ability to "slingshot" out of a curve while leading the pack. This creates a problem for the rest of the field, constantly placing them in the position of having to catch up. Do it enough times in a race and you can grind the field into submission before the decisive last lap.

## INDOOR SPRINTING

A sprinter who wishes to do well indoors knows that the start is the most critical part of the race. As we pointed out in Chapter 3, most world-class sprinters reach maximum velocity between 60 and 70 meters before they begin to decelerate. In most short sprints run indoors on a straight track, the normal racing distance is _50 to 60_ *yards.* Therefore, sprinters who use the bunch start would seem to have an advantage because of their faster block clearance (although there are no comprehensive data suggesting that this method is better).

We do not recommend that sprinters who use a longer pad spacing outdoors shorten the distance between blocks for the indoor sprints. The biomechanics of sprint starts vary with different pad spacing, so a sprinter should practice and use the same start in all sprints rather than make a change for one type of race. Since starting excellence is a product of repeated efforts in training, changes in technique — even for a short time — can upset the rhythm and pattern of a sprinter's running.

*Carlos Lopes's cross-country strength translates into great track and road performances. (Photograph by Alex Pineda / Sailer; courtesy* Track and Field News)

# NINE

# Cross-Country Training and Racing

IF YOU'RE NOT ALREADY racing cross-country, you're missing a good bet. Cross-country combines the best aspects of a wide variety of training techniques. You will need the aerobic endurance and sense of pace you have cultivated in your road racing. You will need the power and ability to accelerate that you have developed in your track racing. And you will need — above all — whatever tactical skills you have learned in all your racing, because cross-country is the quintessential tactical event.

You will never get a PR on a cross-country course; the best ones are designed to discourage all the runner's tricks of smooth, economical striding to maximize efficiency. In good cross-country courses you're constantly accelerating, decelerating, climbing, pounding downhill, running across a slope, jumping a log or a hay bale or a stream.

For many years the world's best coaches have used cross-country training as a regular part of the training of their athletes: not only distance runners, but sprinters, hurdlers, jumpers, throwers, and decathletes, from the high school level to Olympic class. In part, the benefits stem from the physical aspects of cross-country training (which can be demanding), but many of cross-country's benefits to the athlete come from the psychological freedom of training away from the track in "the great outdoors."

Herb Elliott, Olympic 1,500-meter champion in 1960, felt that his cross-country training — year-round, in his case — allowed him to break away from many natural self-imposed limits. Through it, he was able to achieve a physical and mental relaxation that he used on the track in his unbeaten career at 1,500 meters and the mile. Billy Mills, who surprised many by winning the Tokyo Olympic 10,000 meters in 1964, had developed a superior cardiovascular system and great mental toughness during his collegiate years as a cross-country specialist at the University of Kansas. (His win didn't surprise me, since I had barely beaten him for the AAU cross-country title four years earlier.) Other world-class runners with roots in cross-country training include the great New Zealand athletes Peter Snell (three middle-distance Olympic gold medals) and Murray Halberg (Olympic gold at 5,000 meters in 1960). Both were national cross-country champions. Grete Waitz of Norway (Olympic silver in the 1984 Los Angeles women's marathon) was a cross-country specialist before converting to road racing.

Without a doubt, however, the best example of the benefits of cross-country training and racing is Carlos Lopes of Portugal, three-time world cross-country champion. His training has allowed him to have one of the longest careers in world-class racing, reaching from an Olympic 10,000-meter silver medal in 1976 to an Olympic marathon gold in 1984. In 1985, at the age of thirty-seven, Lopes ran the fastest marathon in history (2:07:14).

## Training for Cross-Country

Obviously, to run cross-country well you have to train for it. Training is a little different from the other types of training you're used to, because while each 5K road race tends to be like every other 5K road race and each lap on a track can be like others, it often happens that one cross-country course is totally unlike any other you may run. To oversimplify, "American" cross-country courses are flat and fast (they may be run on the fairways of a golf course), while "European" cross-country courses tend to have greater terrain variation and to include water hazards. When Scottish mile champion James McLatchie came to the United States to run for a university team, he showed up for the first day of cross-country season with the cross-country shoes he had used in Scotland — ankle-high leather boots with nails driven through the soles — and caused a good deal of amusement among his teammates in short track spikes. Jim got some revenge when he was the race director for the 1976 AAU Cross-Country Championships; he designed a 10,000-meter European-type course on the banks of Houston's Buffalo Bayou (complete with loose, sandy stretches, murderous hills, muddy sections, and narrow, water-filled ditches to jump) on which the world's best runners couldn't break 30 minutes.

As this example indicates, the hard and fast lines between American and European courses are quickly eroding. American courses can be very tough; European courses can be flat and fast, as were the 1985 World Championships in Portugal, in which Zola Budd tied her track time for 5,000 meters.

So, while it is possible to do generalized cross-country training, it is much smarter to train for the type of cross-country course you will be running: very hilly or very flat or in between. But nearly all cross-country courses have hills in them — the 1984 World Championships, run at the flat Meadowlands in New Jersey, even had artificial hills built for the occasion — and you can bet that hill training will help your cross-country racing.

## TRAINING FOR HILLS

Often hill training is treated as a unit. But the skills you need in uphill running are not the same as those you need in downhill, so it is more helpful to divide your hill training into two or three different components.

*Uphill running* primarily requires strength, but aerobic endurance is an important secondary factor. The ratio between the two depends on the steepness and length of the hill; short steep hills require more strength, while long gradual hills make a greater demand on the lungs and heart than on the legs. Shorter runners seem to have a biomechanical advantage in uphill running, primarily because they resist the tendency to overstride, which is a muscle-killer (like pushing too big a gear in bicycling). Taller runners can avoid overstriding by thinking about "spinning up the hill" and by concentrating on their form. Everyone, in fact, can improve his or her everyday running form by running regular uphill semi-sprints, con-

*Ann Bond, Team Etonic, runs hills to develop form, balance, and strength. (Photograph by Robert S. Cozens)*

centrating on leg lift and using powerful arm movements to pop them up the hill — but don't overdo it. Watch out especially for Achilles tendinitis in uphill workouts.

If you happen to live where there are *no* hills to train on, not even highway overpasses, there are a few workouts that will provide some of the same benefits. First, since uphill running is a power event, weight lifting will help. Concentrate primarily on the quadriceps (the front part of the thighs) and the calf muscles. Most of the benefit here will be in muscle strength, with little improvement in aerobic endurance. Running up bleachers (also known as the coach's revenge) will produce both increased power and improved cardiovascular fitness, but it has its drawbacks. First, because your foot plant is flat on each step of the stadium, instead of inclined as it will be in uphill running, the stresses on the calf muscle and Achilles tendon are different from those in cross-country racing and may not prepare your lower legs for the loads they will bear (although the workout for the quadriceps will be very close to that in hill training). Additionally, be sure you don't try to run *down* the bleachers: Not only is there a chance that your tired legs may let you fall, but even worse, the impact as you come down quickly onto each step subjects your knees and thighs to very high momentary stress, which can lead to injury.

Another aspect of uphill training can help you in a race. The time may come when you are running against a competitor who beats you on the roads, while you believe that you are better than he or she on the hills. But since even a hilly cross-country course has more flat than hill, you might still get beaten. In this case, a good strategy is to create some "artificial" hills in the course: When the two of you go up a hill together and reach the flat area on top, maintain the same effort you used in racing up the hill. It will become a surge that your competitor will be forced to follow, and you will have created the aerobic effect of making the hill much longer than it actually is. You will have turned a flat area (your competitor's strength) into a hill, your strong point. (Just be sure you can run all those hills yourself.)

*Downhill running* is a skill unto itself. If you're good at it, you can run easily and pass people; if you're not good at it, you'll be passed by people running half as hard as you are.

Just about the only way to get good at it is to do it: Do it over and over and over until you reach your own rhythm and get comfortable. Tall people seem to have a slight biomechanical advantage here, since they can stretch out a bit, but shorter people can be excellent downhill runners. One of the best downhill racers in the world is Bill Rodgers (five foot nine), who destroyed field after field of competitors going down the slopes of Heartbreak Hill in Boston.

One thing to remember in your practice is to take it easy. You can't learn much about downhill running by pelting down the slope out of control, the way you used to do for fun as a kid. The other important thing is to make sure that your shoes are the most supportive you own. The regular impact of your body on your lead leg is formidable under ordinary circumstances, but in downhill running you're adding the impact of your body's falling another several inches, which can increase the impact by a substantial amount. Thus, any tendency you have to poor biomechanical form, such as pronation or supination, will be exaggerated. Additionally, any biomechanical weakness may show up: bad knees, chondromalacia, tendinitis. And you risk stress fractures. So wear your most supportive shoes; they'll help cut down on the impact and its consequences.

Is it better to train up steep short hills or long gentle ones? *Any* type of hill training will improve your ability to race over hills. But if you have a choice, pick hills to train on like those you'll be racing over. Short steep hills are ideal for power runners (more like track racing), while long gentle hills require good aerobic ability (like the long road races). Ideally, train a little over the course itself — that will give you the right kind of hill training and will help you feel at home during the race as well. Unless you're very strong mentally, though, don't train on the course every day; that can lead to a ho-hum feeling that will rob you of some adrenaline when the gun goes off.

*Good hill-running form* is very much like good running form, period. (It might be a good idea to refer to this sentence several times as you read the description below. Nothing in the next paragraphs should lead you to run in a way that looks or feels awkward, strange, or funny.)

A runner starting uphill will probably shorten his or her stride slightly (unless it is ordinarily very compact). Good hill runners will combine that with a slightly higher knee lift, and with a slightly more powerful arm swing, which lets the upper body do part of the uphill work.

While under ordinary road-running circumstances you are striving to maintain pace and to run even splits, neither of these bits of advice applies in hilly cross-country training and racing. If you maintain pace uphill, you will kill yourself off; if you try to run even splits, you will either kill yourself off or run too slowly. You *will* slow down running uphill; if you don't, it's because you were running too slowly to start with (otherwise you'd go into heavy oxygen debt). How much should you slow down? That depends upon the hill, the temperature, the humidity, and the condition of the ground. The best rule of thumb is to try to run with a consistent *effort*: Make the effort used in running up the hill correspond to the effort you just used on the flat approaching the hill.

In training to prepare for what to do once you reach the top of the hill, you have two choices: If you want to be able to surge at the hill-top to kill off your race competition, you may want to put a few such surges into your hill-training sessions. Or, to train to run in the most efficient way, you should instead gradually accelerate as you recover from the stress of the climb. Here again, you'll keep the effort consistent; the increase in speed comes as your body recovers naturally. If your training includes both surging and maintaining techniques, you will then be able to use them when you need them in competition, as your tactical judgment tells you when to race and when to pace.

*Good downhill form* is good running form plus a slightly lower arm carriage. Concentrate on relaxation and balance rather than on leaning forward and barreling down the hill. Let gravity do the work. Your center of gravity should be directly over each foot plant, but you may have to lean *slightly backward* to have it work correctly, depending upon the steepness of the hill.

*Good balance* means having your center of gravity directly over the planted foot at *all* times — as soon as your body deviates from this position, you must use other muscles to keep yourself from falling. (The exception to this rule is in uphill running, when your center of gravity may be slightly forward). Because of this, if your cross-country form is poor, you will fatigue much more quickly than you would on track or road, and more important, you may tire more quickly than your competitors who have better form.

Many cross-country courses have soft and boggy stretches, sometimes combined with uneven ground. In this terrain the runner must reduce his stride length and slightly "chop" his steps if he wishes to keep his weight over his planted foot. Often, however, long-striding and smooth-running track and road runners are unaware of the need for this adjustment. Even if they can hold their pace through this rough running environment, they often expend so much effort maintaining their normal running action that they fall off the pace after successfully negotiating a "horror" stretch on the course.

The best method for handling mud and soft, spongy ground seems to be to shorten stride a bit, slightly increase running cadence, lift the knees a little higher, and think of running over an area strewn with broken glass. Your feet should pat the course; you should be light as a feather and float over the running surface.

The prospective cross-country runner may easily experiment and develop a good rhythm. Find a muddy stretch, put on your oldest shoes, and go to it. The two keys are balance and cadence. After you've hit on something that seems to work for you, try running through the mud with an exaggerated longer stride. You will find that the power you try to put into springing forward is often spent sinking your trailing foot into the mud, and you may have to return to pick up your shoe as well.

*CROSS-COUNTRY PSYCHOLOGY*

We have already discussed the benefits you will gain in physical ability from cross-country training, and — on the other hand — the way in which your road- and track-racing skills can be used to help make the transition to cross-country running. But there is an important additional element you will need to master before you can do your best running in this type of competition: commitment.

The most successful cross-country runners, like the most successful indoor runners, are those who refuse to treat the event as a tune-up or training for another season that is coming later. When you're running a cross-country season, become a cross-country runner and nothing else for that season. Instead of dreading a series of hills, turn them into an opportunity to break your opposition.

There are a number of recognized hill specialists who may be one of the pack on level ground but become "animals" — in the eyes of their opponents — when the ground slopes up. One such runner is Chester Carl, a thirty-two-year-old Navajo who is a three-time winner of the Pike's Peak Ascent. Relaxation and simplicity are the keys to his philosophy of running hills. Uphill, he consciously shortens his stride and leans slightly forward, being careful not to bend from the waist and thus interfere with his breathing. His arm action is a modified sprinter's motion.

He makes it a point to surge over the top of a hill, because he feels most runners have a tendency to ease back as they approach the summit, just as some sprinters will coast through the tape. His downhill action uses lower arm carriage. The one unusual aspect of his running is that he does not lean back during steep descents and

*Chester Carl, hill-running specialist, winning at Pike's Peak —
14,109 feet. (Photograph by David Denney,* Colorado Springs Sun*)*

dig his heels in, preferring to stab his toes into the ground for several steps. Most runners would find this suicidal, but there is no doubt it works for Chester Carl.

Except for this last minor item, it is clear that Chester Carl's hill form is good — but no better than that of hundreds of other runners. Why does he win? Because he believes in his ability to relax and maintain, when others doubt themselves. "I do not attack the hill," he says. "I let the hill come to me. And I know that if I run it right, the hill will set up my competition to be broken."

# A TRACK AND CROSS-COUNTRY GLOSSARY: "HOW MANY TIMES AROUND MAKES A LAP?" AND OTHER DUMB QUESTIONS

BECAUSE MOST OF THE RUNNING BOOM took place on the roads, American runners quickly learned a vocabulary that reflected the training and competition of road races. While some of those terms carry over to track and cross-country racing, enough differences exist in the vocabulary to make a glossary useful.

There is also a substantial body of information that may be new to the novice track runner. The runner who has had high school or collegiate experience will be familiar with much of this, but even these veteran runners may have only general information, not specific.

*Bell lap.* See "Gun lap."

*Benchmark.* A workout or a race that tells the runner he or she meets some previously determined standard for future performance. See discussion in Chapter 2.

*Bludger.* Australian dialect for "one who refuses to work." Thus, distance runners' term for "sprinter."

*Box.* In track racing, a runner is "in a box" when he is in the inside lane and there are runners ahead of him and to his outside. He is thus prevented from accelerating either to take the lead or to cover (*q.v.*) the moves of an opponent. A feared predicament.

*Break.* A runner "gets a break" on his opposition when he moves ahead of them some distance. Exactly how many meters it takes to establish a break depends more on psychological factors than on anything else; it occurs when the pack feels, "It'll be hard to catch him now."

*Contact.* Keeping close to a lead runner; when you lose contact, your opponent has gotten a break on you.

*Cover.* To duplicate a move made by an opponent; for example, if your primary competition picks up the pace with two laps to go, you may wish to pick up your own pace and sit (*q.v.*) on him, thus "covering his move." Covering prevents being caught in a box.

*False start.* If a runner leaves his marks with either hand or foot before the gun is fired, or is felt to have gained an unfair advantage, he will be charged with a false start and the race will be restarted. If detected in time, a false start will be followed by the command "Stand up" (*q.v.*) to the field; if a false start is detected as the gun is fired, a recall (*q.v.*) will be fired. Before the restart, the starter rules which runners were involved in the false start. In high school and college competition, one false start disqualifies a runner; in most other competition two are required for disqualification.

*Fartlek running.* A nonstructured, untimed interval workout. Most road runners already know this term, from the Finnish words for "speed" and "play." A runner will interject brief periods of faster running into an easy workout, usually on grass or another soft surface. He will run "by feel" — speeding up and slowing down for the fun of it.

*Field.* As in horse racing, all the contestants in a race. Also, as in the phrase "track and field," the nonrunning events (such as pole vault, javelin, et al.).

*Gun lap.* The last lap in a multilap race, so called because a starting pistol is fired when the race leader passes the finish line with only one more lap to go. In England and on the Continent (where they are more sensible about firearms), a bell is rung instead; hence "bell lap."

*Hare.* See *Rabbit.*

*Harrier.* Originally any animal that chases rabbits or hares; a breed of dog is known by this name. Hence a slang term for any cross-country runner. Thence a popular name for running clubs in the British Commonwealth; e.g., Botany Harriers. Since other dog breeds also chase rabbits, other club names suggested themselves, some of which sound strange to North American ears: Midfifties marathon great Jim Peters ran for the Essex Beagles.

*Kick.* Sprinting ability.

*Lapped.* To be caught from behind, and passed, in a race by someone who is ahead of you. The worst way to reestablish contact.

*Metric tracks.* Nearly all new outdoor tracks are 400 meters long; many older tracks were built to the English standard of 440 yards. Since the two distances are only about one-half of 1 percent different (400 meters is 99.42 percent of 440 yards), most of the suggested times given in the training schedules in this book are valid for either type of track. Even four laps on a metric track (1,600 meters) is close enough to a mile (1,609.3 meters) for training purposes; you'll be within 2 seconds of a true mile. If you feel guilty about it, run one of your laps in Lane 2 and thereby pick up an extra 8 yards.

*Pack.* The group of lead or near-lead runners, running together to conserve energy and to keep an eye on each other. (Also a road-racing term.)

*Pole.* To be "on the pole" in track running means to be running in the inside lane, usually in front. It is not necessarily to have the fastest time in qualifying (as it is in auto racing).

*Rabbit.* A runner who paces other runners in a multilap track race; the understanding is that the rabbit will set the pace for the first half or three-quarters of the race and then drop out or slow to a jog and let the "real" runners compete. (Not to be confused with a front-runner, who will be trying to win the race.)

If as a race field lines up, you see three or four outstanding milers and one runner who is a great quarter- and half-miler, you will be justified in suspecting that there will be a rabbit in the race. Generally, such pacing is considered illegal, especially for record consideration. Nevertheless, rabbits are widely used on the major European racing circuit, where promoters can attract a crowd with the promise of a fast race or a record attempt; there a good rabbit can even command a sizable fee for his work. In practice, most records set with a rabbit's assistance are allowed to stand. One notable exception is in women's track races: For record consideration, the presence of men on the track may be ruled to constitute illegal pacing (even if the men are competing in their own race).

*Recall.* If one runner "false starts" (*q.v.*), a second shot will be fired immediately after the shot that starts the race. The two gunshots signal a recall.

*Relays.* Relays, among the most exciting track events, are run in a wide variety. The Olympic events, and the relays most often run, are the 4 × 400-meter and the 4 × 100-meter relays. Additionally, there is a wide range of 4 × various distances (200, 800, 1,500, mile), as well as the sprint medley (200, 100, 100, 400 for women; 200, 200, 400, 800 for men), and the distance medley (400, 800, 1,200, 1,600). There are even such esoterica as the shuttle hurdle relays, in which a hurdler runs 110 meters over hurdles in one direction and hands off to another, who hurdles back again in the opposite direction, and so on.

*Rig.* A feeling like muscle paralysis, caused by fatigue and metabolic changes in the muscle during intense anaerobic effort. Marathoners have "the wall"; sprinters have "the bear," which jumps on your back about 80 percent of the way through any sprint. "Rig" is derived from rigor mortis, which probably describes the feeling as clearly as any attempt at a fuller definition. Also called "tying up."

*Rolling.* A risky type of start in which the sprinter, without moving his hands or feet, begins to move his body forward just before he thinks he will hear the starting gun. If he has anticipated correctly, and if he is undetected by the starter, he will have a slight advantage in the race. If he is caught, he will be charged with a false start and the race will be restarted. If the gun doesn't come at the anticipated time, he must either false start or fall on his face. Sometimes a starter will catch a runner rolling and delay the pistol a split second to see what will happen.

*Sit.* To run close behind another runner or just behind his outside shoulder. This is the tactic of choice when you are sure your kick (*q.v.*) is better than the other runner's, and you can thus hang on to him or her until the final 200 meters, then pass and win. "Sit in," a training term, means to accompany: "Why don't you sit in with me on this quarter?" The implication is that the speaker will set the pace.

*Sitter.* One who uses the tactic of sitting. The term sometimes is derogatory, since a sitter, it is universally felt, doesn't do the work a lead runner does but acts more as a parasite. Because sitting is perceived to be a favorite tactic of British runners, there are parts of the world where the term Pommy sitter (although redundant) is considered an insult.

*Speed through the back door.* A training technique in which the runner increases his sprinting ability by practicing surges (*q.v.*) of 50 to 150 meters in the course of longer, easier runs. Similar to fartlek training, except that the surges are planned and executed on a scheduled basis, not dictated by feel.

*"Stand up."* Command given by the starter when the commands "On your marks" and "Set" cannot be followed by the gun. This can occur for a number of reasons: a runner losing his balance while leaning forward in a distance race (you must be "steady on the mark"), unreadiness of the timing crew, a hurdle on the track, or a misfire of the starting pistol. Most runners will jog a second or two to loosen up before getting ready to take their marks again.

*Strength.* A term with several meanings in running, some of which may seem directly contradictory. (1) Strength can mean the muscular power you gain from lifting weights. This power helps primarily in the short-distance "explosive" events (e.g., the sprints). (2) Strength — as used in events from the half-mile on up — can also mean the ability to maintain a high level of stress and moderate oxygen debt over an extended period of time. Thus, although sprint speed is largely a product of muscle strength (definition 1), it is entirely possible for a sprinter to lack the strength (definition 2) to be a good miler.

Perhaps all this is made even more confusing by the often-quoted training philosophy of Pat Clohessy and his protégé Rob de Castella: "speed through strength." Here not only does strength mean endurance, but speed does not mean anything like sprinting ability, but rather the ability to maintain a *faster* pace *longer* than the other guy can. Some people would also call this endurance. At any rate, "speed through strength" sounds better than "endurance through endurance." And, needless to say, it works just fine for de Castella.

*Stagger.* (1) What you may do at the end of a track race if you go out too fast. (2) The different starting positions for sprints that are run around the curve. The staggered start is necessary to ensure that all runners in these races run the same distance and finish at the same line. Staggered starts make it difficult to judge the leader in early stages of 200-meter and 400-meter races, because the competitors are not running even with each other until they leave the final turn. Logically, the staggers are twice as long for a 400-meter race (about 8 yards) as for a 200-meter race (about 4). When a runner "makes up the stagger" on an opponent, that means that he is running shoulder to shoulder with the competitor in the next lane outside. By making up the several yards of the stagger, the inside runner may be having a great race, or he may have gone out too fast. (See definition 1).

*Surge.* A period of acceleration during a race or a training interval in which the pace is increased for a distance (usually 50 to 150 meters), followed by slowing down to the earlier pace.

*Tailor-made.* A coaching term describing a runner whose form is deliberately a composite of the best parts of other runners' actions; characteristic of a high degree of biomechanical sophistication. Valery Borzov, the great Soviet sprinter, is perhaps the outstanding example.

*Timing.* There are a number of conventions used to indicate times in track racing and training. Hand-timed (HT) competitions are not supposed to be reported in hundredths of seconds, even though most current watches will provide that information; the time recorded should be rounded up to the next tenth. A time of 12.03 in a hand-timed 100-meter dash should be reported as 12.1. Only times produced by fully automatic timing (FAT), in which the clock is activated by the starter's gun and the final time is read by an automatic device, should be reported and printed in hundredths. Thus, a printed report of Steve Cram's 1,500-meter record of 3:29.67 immediately tells a reader that FAT conditions were observed. Semi-automatic timing, in which the clock is either started or stopped by an automatic device (but not both), is more subject to human error and thus should be rounded up to the next tenth. (Old races timed with mechanical stopwatches are often given to ¼ or ⅕ second: Walter George's 1886 mile record is 4:12¾.)

It is usually assumed that a given sprint will seem faster HT than FAT — a 10.2 HT might well be a 10.43 FAT, for example. For converting HT to FAT, the rule of thumb suggested by *Track and Field*

*News* is to add 0.24 for races of less than one lap, 0.14 for races of one lap.

Should you be asked to time a race, start your watch when you see the flash or smoke from the starter's pistol; don't wait for the sound. Stop your watch at the instant your runner's torso (not arms, legs, or head) touches the vertical plane above the edge of the finish line.

*Track.* Not only the running oval; when shouted, the word means "I am coming up quickly behind you; please move out of my lane." Ordinarily used only in training, but may be worth trying in a race.

# *AFTERWORD*

In 1936, it would have been inconceivable that someone would one day run fast enough to beat the great Jesse Owens by more than 5 yards in the 100. Yet such a performance has today become almost commonplace, partly because of technological improvements in tracks and equipment, but largely through progress in the theory and practice of training — progress that takes into account breakthroughs in physiology, sports psychology, and biomechanics. In *The Self-Coached Runner II,* Mark Scheid and Allan Lawrence have combined the findings of these decades of coaching experience and training development with practical training blueprints for improvement at all levels: high school, college, open, master's, and corporate.

In the future, as our sport progresses, it will become essential that *runners* as well as coaches become aware of the information in this book. It will no longer suffice for runners to follow blindly their coach's instructions, because even sprinters will need to make split-second decisions during a race. In essence, so that the standards of our sport will continue to improve, all competitors will need to become "self-coached runners."

Tom Tellez
1984 U.S. Olympic Sprint Coach

# INDEX